MODZINES

MODZINES

FANZINE CULTURE FROM THE MOD REVIVAL

EDDIE PILLER AND STEVE ROWLAND

OMNIBUS PRESS

London / New York / Paris / Sydney / Copenhagen / Berlin / Madrid / Tokyo

fanzine   noun / 'fæn.ziːn/
Also zine. A non-professional and non-official
publication produced by enthusiasts of a
particular cultural phenomenon (such as a
literary or musical genre) for the pleasure
of others who share their interest. Fanzine
is a compound of both 'fan' and 'magazine'.

CONTENTS

MODZINES INTRODUCTION

I am writing this book because back in 1979, while still at school and before I took my O-levels, I became inspired by a brand-new cultural phenomenon, or rather an old cultural phenomenon rehashed for the post-punk generation. It was an idea that transcended the norms of what passed for popular culture at the time, but it seemed to embrace a new vision, a vision that I felt a part of. Paul Weller called it the Modern World. The media called it the mod revival.

The story begins at least a year before I started my own fanzine, *Extraordinary Sensations*. I had been an avid reader of *Maximum Speed*, the first of the mod fanzines to appear at gigs, East End pubs and occasionally on the terraces of Upton Park in the early days of 1979. It spoke to me and my friends in a way the music papers never quite managed to do. It told me when, where and how. The mod scene was an ever-thrusting force for a 15-year-old in late 1978/early 1979, and a trio of fanzines educated me, enlightened me and manipulated me to see the world in the way I wanted, or rather needed, to see it. But *Maximum Speed* was most definitely the first. And the best.

For a year or so I had followed the mainstream music media – *Sounds*, the *New Musical Express* and *Melody Maker* – but gradually I felt disenfranchised. The middle-aged staff writers on the inkies had nothing to say to me. They could hardly relate to The Jam or Buzzcocks, let alone Purple Hearts, The Chords or Secret Affair, so eventually I gave up reading them.

Instead, I sought out the home-made magazines *Maximum Speed*, *Shake* and *Direction Reaction Creation*. They illustrated and illuminated the path I wanted to follow, that of the mod revival. Why? Well, it was because they covered my world, the music and the clothes I was into. They reviewed my bands, the ones I went to watch on a wet Tuesday in Highgate or in a crap pub up the Balls Pond Road in the middle of the week.

Eventually, the originators of these first mod fanzines lost interest and towards the end of '79 I noticed a lull in their commitment and the regularity of their publication.

Around the same time, I met Tony Lordan and Vaughn Toulouse [of the mod/ska band Guns For Hire, later to morph into Department S], who were editing the modzine *Get Up And Go!*. They sold me a copy (Issue 2, since you ask) at a Small Hours gig at the Rock Garden during the closing months of '79. The pair of them could not have been more encouraging and helpful, so six months later, I decided to take the plunge.

I made only 20 copies of Issue 1 of *Extraordinary Sensations* (the name came from a Purple Hearts live tune, which eventually made it on to the B-side of their classic 45 'Frustration'). I photocopied them at my dad's shop – bear in mind I was still at school – and sold each one for 20p at a gig by the Leyton-based Welsh mod band Beggar, who were playing at the Bridge House Hotel in Canning Town on a rainy Monday night. Stupidly, I never kept a copy and so will probably never own a full set of the 16 *Extraordinary Sensations* issues that made it into circulation.

By Issue 2, I had persuaded a friend to use a copier at his work. Issue 3 was made with some really weird drum-type printer at my mum's office (although I made 50 copies, they appeared to be printed on blotting paper!). By Issue 4, I had found a mate who was prepared to run off copies at his print shop when the boss wasn't looking. From that point on, there was no looking back.

Letraset, PMT machines, typewriters, and cut and paste are long gone and never to return. But my love of the world of ramshackle, amateur and cobbled-together magazines that I once inhabited has never left me. Eventually, Terry Rawlings joined me in the *Extraordinary Sensations* office (in Ernie Brain's Haulage Yard in Dagenham) and between us we released a total of 16 issues and one compendium of some of the best bits, which we titled *A Legal Matter (The Mod Guide to Sex)*. Sales peaked with 15,000 with Issue 14 and *Extraordinary Sensations* enjoyed a successful run that only came to an end when Stiff Records came on the scene and offered us our own record label.

Eddie Piller

Extraordinary Sensations –
Eddie Piller and Terry
Rawlings, Essex 1981.
Maximum Speed – Goffa
Gladding, Clive Reams and
Kim Gault, London 1979.
Shake – Dom Kenny and Mike,
London 1980. Get Up and Go
– Tony Lordan and Vaughn
Toulouse, London 1979.

Part One:
The First
Mod Revival

MOD TAKES OVER

Sniffin Glue – Mark
Perry, London 1976
48 Thrills – Adrian
Thrills, Essex 1976

No other youth culture or subculture centred on fashion or music, or both, has ever had as many fanzines dedicated to it as the mod revival. Punk might well have started the concept but the world of the mods arrived at the juncture of a perfect storm. The lack of mainstream press coverage combined with the ease of production and an enormous and voracious young public – from the West Coast of America to rural Japan, or a mining village in Derbyshire to a wild-west border outpost in Northern Ireland – made modzines a truly global phenomenon.

It is impossible to know exactly how many different mod fanzines were published at any one time because a good amount only ran for one or two issues before their creators lost interest or moved on to something else. Some were produced in such limited numbers that they may never have made it outside of the editor's town, village or even circle of friends. *Extraordinary Sensations* Issue 1 is lost to posterity for precisely this reason. I only made 20 copies, nearly all of which would have ended up in someone's bin within 24 hours!

However, I would estimate that well over a thousand titles have been produced since the mod revival kicked off. Some endured in the popular consciousness but many did not, and were cast aside because they were simply (and intentionally) disposable.

Fanzines sprung up as a direct consequence of the do-it-yourself attitude of those early punk-rock pioneers back in late 1976 and early 1977. Mark Perry's *Sniffin' Glue* was probably the first of its kind, but, to be honest, not many people were taking notes back then. However, the fanzine soon became the ultimate disposable journalistic torpedo, fired into the bow of the vessel that was the old school and established music press. And the two that had arguably the biggest impact were *48 Thrills* and *Jamming!*.

Enthusiastic teenager Adrian Thrills created the zine that carried his name. Swept along with the excitement of bands like The Clash, The Jam and the Sex Pistols, who he'd seen over the summer of '76 at the 100 Club* and other pub venues, Adrian remembers where it all began.

"I did the first issue of *48 Thrills* in September 1976. I was at college in Harlow in Essex and the London punk scene was inspiring – and virtually on my doorstep. The bands were accessible and there was a great sense of mutual support. This was before any tabloid punk pieces, or the infamous Bill Grundy TV interview with the Pistols, so the scene was still underground. There were a couple of switched-on journalists, like John Ingham and Caroline Coon, who were covering the scene in the weekly papers, but the only punk fanzine at that point was *Sniffin' Glue*. I got to know *SG* editor Mark P, and he encouraged me to have a go myself.

"*48 Thrills* was part of that first wave of punk fanzines. It was a chance for me to reflect on and become engaged in the scene. I had no plans to make

*The 100 Club is a London music venue located at 100 Oxford Street. Over the years, it has played host to beat, punk rock, mod, jazz, soul and R&B bands, including hosting the first-ever international punk festival in September 1976, which featured, among others, the Sex Pistols, Buzzcocks and The Clash.

a career out of writing about music at that stage. I wrote the first issue in a single morning, printed off 10 copies on the Xerox machine in the local library and sold them all at a gig the same night.

"I did six issues in total, the second one coming out very soon after the first. The last one arrived in September 1977, 12 months after I started."

48 Thrills set the distribution template that just about every fanzine editor has followed since, but Adrian was also one of the first to discover that fanzines are not a good way to make money, but that wasn't what mattered.

"I sold the fanzine mainly at gigs, but a few via post once the punk gospel had spread beyond London. Some shops also took them – Geoff Travis at Rough Trade was supportive, as was Don Letts, who ran [the clothing store] Acme Attractions on the Kings Road. By the final issue, my print run had grown from the 10 copies I did for that first one to about 500 for the last. It never made any money, but that wasn't the point. I probably broke even. More importantly, I catalogued some momentous times."

As *48 Thrills* wound down, an even younger Tony Fletcher launched his own fanzine, *Jamming!*, when he was 13 years old.

"I kicked off in late '77 and the inspiration was as simple as seeing Jon Savage's centre-page spread on fanzines in *Sounds* and figuring, that looks like fun!"

What made both *48 Thrills* and *Jamming!* different from the majority of other punk fanzines was that the editors were both influenced and supported by, to some extent at least, The Jam.

Adrian Thrills again: "The Jam were a vital band for me, both as a fan and a writer. Shane MacGowan* and I interviewed them together for the fanzine and Paul Weller was always good at supplying ideas. He plugged *48 Thrills* onstage at the Marquee, and even helped out on a practical level. He, Rick and Bruce helped to staple together the individual sheets for one issue while they were making their debut album at Polydor Studios in Stratford Place in the West End. I turned up straight from a nearby photocopying shop and we spread hundreds of sheets of paper over the studio floor and stapled them together between takes of 'Away From The Numbers'."

Tony Fletcher also credits The Jam for their help: "*Jamming!* was definitely a punk-inspired fanzine but I found The Jam enormously supportive. I've often talked about how I wrote to Paul Weller [care of] the fan club in the summer of '78, sent him what was then just a school fanzine, asked for an interview and got a letter back within a week or so inviting me to the studio where they were recording *All Mod Cons*. It was a benchmark moment and I wish that every interview had been as easy to arrange!"

*The ebullient Shane MacGowan was a very early face on the punk scene, editing his own fanzine, *Bondage*, before going on to establish The Nipple Erectors, a famously raucous punk band. They eventually morphed into the mod-influenced Nips, whose 45 'Gabrielle' is one of the forgotten revival classics. Paul Weller produced the Nips single 'Happy Song', but the band split in frustration at their lack of success, and Shane went on to form the enormously successful Pogues.

JAMMING

EXCLUSIVE INTERVIEW WITH

THE JAM

25P   **No.5**

In the studio with Paul Weller. New LP!!

AND MORE EXCLUSIVE INTERVIEWS WITH
ADAM-&-THE-ANTS · JOHN PEEL
READING FESTIVAL · CARNIVAL 2
ULTRAVOX · BE-BOP DELUXE + LOTS MORE

48 Thrills – Adrian
Thrills, Essex 1976
Jamming – Tony
Fletcher, London 1978–9

Paul Weller himself remembers: "I generally can't stand anything that is too 'mainstream', so it's the smaller, more underground things I tend to look for. I like people who aren't swayed by the obvious, it makes it more real for me… that's why I liked – and continue to like – fanzines…"

By the end of 1978, a new style of teenage fashion, also inspired by The Jam, was emerging on the football terraces and in the pubs and clubs of London. The wearers called themselves 'mods', and while they had little in common with their sixties forebears, they grasped at the iconography of that long-vanished youth cult and adopted it as their own. The US Army parka, the trilby hat, the Harrington jacket, desert or monkey boots and a Fred Perry T-shirt made up the basic look. Small pockets of adherents sprung up in certain areas, like East London, Paddington and Waterloo, and as they grew in number, these new mods began to coalesce into a scene.

But the new mod scene didn't just appear whole; it took a while to evolve from the ever-increasing mess of what had once been a thrusting and vibrant punk scene only a year earlier.

Roger Allen, himself the editor of a punk fanzine, **The Surrey Vomet**, recalls the early false starts before the mod revival finally found its feet.

"1976 was the year I thought it was all going to happen. I was 17 and had just bought my first Lambretta. Bands were emerging like Dr Feelgood, Eddie & The Hot Rods and the Flamin' Groovies, all playing short two- or three-minute songs with a definite sixties look and vibe. I guess I saw it as a backlash against all those seventies loon-wearing, 20-minute guitar-soloing hippies. I drove my scooter down to Bizarre Records on Praed Street in Paddington, where I knew they were selling 'Wooly Bully' by Eddie & The Hot Rods and unbelievably there was another Lambretta parked outside the shop! But it wasn't anything like a 'mod revival'.

"(Then), in 1977, The Jam came on the scene and I definitely thought that the mod revival really was born. The press called it 'punk' and tried to disparage the mod-influenced Dr Feelgood by calling the band 'pub rock', as if that term somehow cheapened them. I had the *Nuggets* compilation album from 1973, which showcased the original 'sixties punk rock' and included some of my favourite bands like The Standells and The Seeds, so I was happy with the more credible title 'punk' that had been awarded to those bands the papers did approve of. I was even happy with some of the bands that didn't quite fit into my vision of what a mod revival should have been, like the Sex Pistols."

"I brought out a fanzine in '78, which I called **The Surrey Vomet** [a pun on the local rag *The Surrey Comet*]. It was full of sixties imagery, like photos of Brian Jones and Marianne Faithfull, and cuttings from classic comics. Then Generation X released 'Ready Steady Go', in which they sung about being in love with Cathy McGowan! Things seemed to be on a roll.

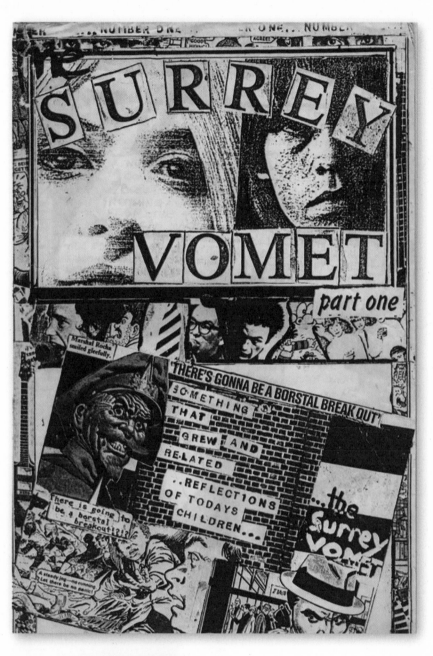

Surrey Vomet - Roger Allen, Surrey 1978.
Can't Explain - Roger Allen, Surrey 1979.
Fanzine editor Roger Allen.

Jamming – Tony Fletcher, London 1979.
Can't Explain – Roger Allen, Surrey 1979.
Go Go – Jackie Topham and Bernadine Wood, Dagenham Essex 1985.

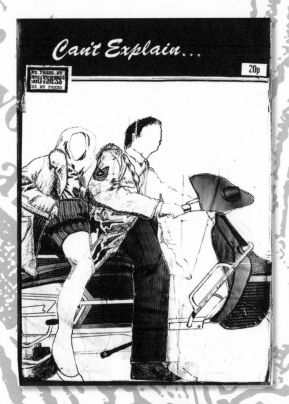

"But it turned out it wasn't the 'mod revival' proper. Slowly the whole scene was being pushed along to a leather-jacketed, motorcycle boot-wearing world, which I didn't want to be a part of. Then came along the skinhead revival/Sham 69 thing, which I took to be putting a brake on the art school excesses of punk, but it still wasn't 'mod' as I had imagined it. Punk had turned from being an energetic 'you can do anything/set up your own record label/bring out your own magazine' vibe to become this Mohican-wearing, depressant-taking, turgid 'I hate everything' scene I wanted nothing to do with."

And Roger wasn't alone; by the middle of 1978, many of the younger punks had become disillusioned and felt disenfranchised.

Bernadine Wood, who later became joint editor of the early eighties mod fanzine *GoGo* with her friend Jackie Topham, remembers: "I got into the mod scene in late 1978. I'd been going to loads of punk gigs and loved the energy of live music, but the fashion simply didn't appeal. Gradually I started to see a few smarter-dressed people at gigs, like when The Jam played at the Music Machine or Generation X at the Marquee, and that was pretty much it. I was never really a punk – from that point on, I was a mod."

Bands, too, were rejecting the standard punk ethos. Paul Weller of The Jam had been a self-declared mod since school, Buzzcocks and Generation X flirted with the imagery and Clem Burke from New York pop-punk pioneers Blondie adopted the fashion. Many of these band members and aspiring mod punters had picked up the attitude themselves from the pages of the gatefold edition of Pete Townshend's 1973 rock opera *Quadrophenia*, which upon its release had been accompanied by a 16-page photo-story of a young mod living the dream. The early revival mods wanted some of that for themselves.

Adrian Thrills, who had by this time swapped his fanzine for a journalistic career, soon noticed this nascent movement.

"I became aware of the mod revival in late 1978 and started writing about it the following year. I was at **NME** by then and covered a lot of the mod bands on the London circuit – The Chords, Purple Hearts, The Merton Parkas, Nine Below Zero, The Lambrettas, Long Tall Shorty, The Fixations and Secret Affair. I did a big mod revival piece, a cover story, for the paper in April 1979."

Tony Fletcher, whose *Jamming!* was fast assuming the elements of a proper and credible magazine, also felt some solidarity with the new scene. "As *Jamming!* was so irregular and sporadic, I tackled lots of aspects of the revival in one fell swoop at some point over the summer of 1979, with a long analysis/editorial as part of a new band special that featured The Chords, Speedball and The Teenbeats.

"I was, however, conflicted. On the one hand I loved the mod revival because it was the culture I'd always wanted to be a part of – had I been able to tell God I wanted to be born in about 1948 and not 1964! But it was such a bandwagon from the moment I dropped into it and it was evident from the beginning that it was lacking the individuality that surely marked the original movement as being so effective and positive. It seemed to have very little time to incubate before it had swept the suburbs and it was all over. Frankly, I always thought that the term 'modernist revival' was an oxymoron. However, at the age of 15 I had no idea of the word oxymoron's existence, let alone its meaning, so I'm being a complete revisionist here!"

While *Jamming!* viewed the revival from the perspective of an enthusiastic outsider, the first mod fanzines were taking control of their own world.

Brett 'Buddy' Ascott, drummer with The Chords – one of the first new mod bands on the scene – said, "Enthusiasm will always fill a vacuum. If punk was swiftly overtaken and exploited by Svengalis and managers then mod never was. If anything, it was a reaction against that. It was genuinely from the streets and that was why the mainstream media took against it."

Younger teenagers had firmly rejected the fake-anarchy antics of Malcolm McLaren and the Sid 'n' Nancy brigade. The internal punk battle between art-house and boot-boy rock was building but becoming increasingly irrelevant to the next generation. Kings Road poster boys with their green Mohicans and studded leather jackets looked ridiculous, so just where could these disillusioned kids turn? The answer for many was mod.

And why not? A reimagining of Britain's most successful and legendary youth culture, which had peaked just 13 years earlier and maintained stubborn outposts of style that clung on until the early seventies, was a natural progression for many. In place of the £350 bondage trousers from clothes store Boy came second-hand Tonik* suits and parkas from jumble sales and army surplus stores. It was a cheap look and easy to identify, and identify with.

Roger Allen again: "If you stay true to your ideals you eventually meet other like-minded people. The first proper mod/scooter scene that I found was in Southend in 1978. The Southend Quadrophonics [named after The Who album, not the film, which hadn't been released at this point] were a scooter club who Rob, of the early revival band Speedball, introduced me to. Speedball were getting into the mod thing after playing some local gigs with Purple Hearts. By the beginning of '79 the mod revival was picking up speed. Along with Speedball and the Quadrophonics, I travelled along to the Bishop's Stortford Mod Festival, which was where I met Goffa and Clive, two of the editors of the first ever mod fanzine, *Maximum Speed.*"

Many regard that gig, which was held at the Triad Centre in the Hertfordshire market town of Bishop's Stortford in May 1979, as the real starting point of

*Tonik, occasionally referred to as Two-Tone, was a cross-weaved fabric, usually a blend of wool and mohair, first invented in the 1960s. Tonik suits were quickly adopted by mods, who loved the way the fabric appeared to shimmer or change colour in the light.

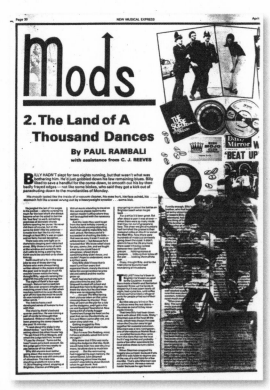

Maximum Speed – Goffa Gladding, Clive Reams
and Kim Gault, London 1979.
New Musical Express.
Grant Flemming, Paris 1979 as featured
in Maximum Speed.
Bishop Stortford 'Mod Festival'.

Grant Flemming, Paris 1979.
Adrian Thrills - New Musical Express.
Mods Mayday '79 LP - Bridge House Records

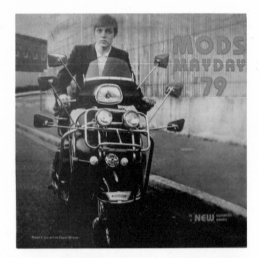

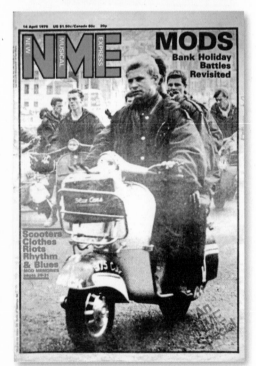

NEW MUSICAL EXPRESS   April 14th, 1979

QUADS?
QUODS?

Who are they and how do you spell it?
ADRIAN THRILLS looks at the sounds
and styles of Modrophenia '79

Reconstructions of the mod lifestyle from The Who's forthcoming 'Quadrophenia' movie. Above: blood and bluebeat hats. Below Life on an LI.

The Chords from Deptford.   Pic: Mike Laye

The Fixations from North London.   Pic: Stevenson

The Purple Hearts from Romford.   Pic: Mike Laye

the revival. For others, like former Sham 69 roadie Grant Fleming, it started three months earlier with a trip to see The Jam in Paris. Whatever the starting point, by the spring of 1979 there was a recognisable scene.

Gary Sparks, drummer with Purple Hearts, remembers: "The Triad Centre was by no means the first mod revival gig but it was the first one that I remember as an arranged 'mod' event – prior to that, bands were just playing where they could and gradually more and more young mod kids were turning up. There was an emerging scene but that Bishop's Stortford gig was the first sort of… Woodstock for mods!"

April and May of that year saw a never-healthier live scene for bands in London; a quick look at the *Sounds* and *NME* gig guides from that period record a plethora of established punk and new wave groups gigging every night, very often with the 16/17-year-old original mod bands supporting.

GoGo's Bernadine Wood again: "In the very early days, the mod scene was extraordinarily vibrant with loads going on, and you could go to a mod-related gig most nights of the week, even if you were just going to see the support band. It was common for our bands to be paired up with completely inappropriate headliners, but, to be honest, we didn't care as we would never hang around to see them."

By late spring of '79, mod groups began headlining their own shows. Among the first and biggest were the aforementioned Chords and Purple Hearts, along with Secret Affair. There were others, too, including The Mods from Borehamwood, Beggar from South Wales and the incredibly soulful Small Hours, who featured a former member of Australian rock band The Saints, the bassist Kym Bradshaw.

Also on the live scene were Squire, a band that hailed from Weller's stomping ground of Woking and indeed included his hairdresser, Enzo Esposito, on guitar and vocals. They joined Secret Affair and some of the other early bands on Bridge House Records' *Mods Mayday '79* live compilation. The album was the first release to stem from the new scene, and it originally included a performance from The Merton Parkas, fronted by Mick and Danny Talbot, who had their appearance curtailed before release following contractual pressure from their new label, Beggars Banquet.

The emerging mod scene revolved around Weller's band The Jam and dozens of other young groups who had sprung up in their wake in late '78 and early '79. The major live residencies were at the Bridge House Hotel in Canning Town (where the *Mods Mayday* album had been recorded during one of their Mod Monday nights), the Wellington pub in Waterloo, the King's Head in Deptford and the Global Village in Charing Cross, which had enthusiastically changed its name to Vespas.

By April 1979, the iconography of mod had more or less solidified. That it was a real and tangible working-class movement from the streets was underlined by the fact that parkas had sprung up on the terraces and, at last, the middle-class music press was taking notice. But not necessarily in the way they would have wanted. When Ian McCulloch, from *Sounds*, finally trekked down to see the Purple Hearts, he slaughtered them in his review. The band didn't receive much love from other mainstream quarters, either.

Purple Hearts guitarist Simon Stebbing recalls when the tide turned: "The mainstream music press had this assumption that we were just re-running the sixties, but as far as I was concerned, we were very seventies, and that's where the punk fanzine ethos comes in. If these magazines were going to understand what we were trying to achieve then it needed people from our own world and of our own age to write it down. Purple Hearts were a combination of mod attitude and punk music, and the mod revival was just a natural progression from punk. The *NME* really slagged us off, saying, 'They sound more like Generation X than The Yardbirds.' I thought fucking hell, Generation X, brilliant. They couldn't understand that we owed more to Generation X than The Yardbirds, because most of the journalists were 40-odd and so out of touch with what was going on in our world that they made loads of sweeping and incorrect assumptions."

It wasn't only the music press that was taking notes; the new movement sparked the interest of leading players in the punk scene too. Tony James and Billy Idol, who had purloined original 1960s mod imagery for their own band, Generation X, went to watch The Chords, Purple Hearts and Back To Zero at the Cambridge Hotel on the North Circular, London, in April. They were quoted as saying they thought the scene was "interesting but safe". Paul Weller, whose band The Jam gave the scene its focus, watched The Chords fifth-ever gig at the Wellington pub in Waterloo, and by doing so, gave the mod revival his blessing, which only amped up interest in the scene. A month later, Weller proclaimed The Chords as his anointed successors and promptly offered them the much-coveted Jam support slot.

The post-Howard Devoto* Buzzcocks had their own internal war, with the art-school influence of Pete Shelley on one side and the out-and-out 'modness' of Steve Diggle on the other. The battle manifested itself in their angular chords and modernist-inspired album sleeve artwork, and by mid-'79 they'd gone off in their own direction, a slightly different 'punk version' of mod.

Perhaps most significant of them all, Jimmy Pursey, lead vocalist of boot-boy punk-chart heroes Sham 69, who was never one to knowingly undersell himself, embraced the mod scene. He set up his own record label, JP Productions, and promptly signed Long Tall Shorty, The Chords and The Low Numbers.

*Howard Devoto was a founder member of Manchester punk rock band Buzzcocks. He left after the release of their first EP, Spiral Scratch, to set up one of the first post-punk bands, Magazine.

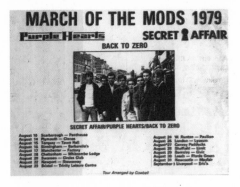

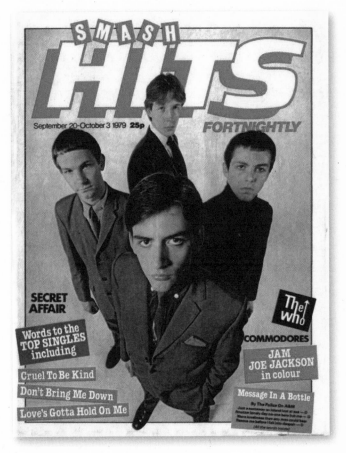

Purple Hearts cover – Melody Maker 1979,
March of the Mods, Secret Affair
cover – Smash Hits 1979,
New Musical Express, Merton Parkas.

Sham's label Polydor initially picked up JP Productions' albums for distribution but, as so often happened with Pursey at that time, politics reared its ugly head.

Pursey and in-house producer Pete Wilson brought The Chords to Polydor Studios to record a demo. Polydor were ecstatic with the end result and called the band back two days later to record their debut single, 'Now It's Gone'. Pursey was so into the concept of mod, he proposed the record be released as a 12-inch single on red, white and blue vinyl. The contract was duly signed.

The Chords should have released the first mod revival single, but fate was to intervene. The band were supporting their good friends The Undertones on their UK tour when, towards the end of May 1979, Pursey arrived at a gig in the Guildford Civic Hall, unannounced, and introduced himself to the unassuming Irish headliners. He asked if he could join them on stage for an encore with his mates, Paul Cook and Steve Jones from the Sex Pistols.

"Surely you lads know my song 'Borstal Breakout'? Let's do that?"

The Undertones, somewhat understandably but as politely as possible, refused the request, which made Pursey apoplectic with rage. As The Undertones set progressed, the charismatic but ultimately flawed punk legend, along with Cook and Jones and a following of around 50 skinheads, edged their way closer to the stage. The confrontation, when it came, was brutal and unforgiving. The Undertones retired to the dressing room, leaving the skinheads in control of the venue. The Chords were mortified. Pursey was, after all, their guest, but he had ruined the gig. The band members were in turmoil and ultimately decided after a long discussion that they couldn't be involved with such a controversial figure. They insisted that Jimmy Pursey cancel the band's contract with JP Productions. At a meeting three days later, an apologetic Pursey agreed to release The Chords from their obligations. The band jumped at the chance but realised they were now in limbo; Polydor had an option to release their record but declined to exercise it. Their contract was shelved.

Jimmy Pursey soon jumped ship from Polydor and The Chords-less JP Productions found a new home with new mentor Dave Dee, who himself had experience of the sixties mod scene through the band Dave Dee, Dozy, Beaky, Mick & Tich. Dee thought Pursey had been onto something so he took the label to Warner Bros., where he was an A&R man.

Tony Perfect, lead singer and guitarist with Long Tall Shorty, picks up the story: "Mark, [our drummer's] mum worked for Jimmy Pursey's manager and suggested that he might appreciate the new mod scene. As soon as he saw us and The Chords he was hooked. Punk was really influenced by the sixties, and Jimmy thought that the growing mod scene was what punk rock should have been (or possibly could have been); very young

and working class, which couldn't have been said about punkers, most of whom were chancers and pub-rock refugees in their late twenties and thirties – our youngest member, bass player Jimmy Grant, was just 15 when we first played at the Marquee. It was the music Pursey had grown up with; all of the revival bands had been influenced to some extent by The Kinks, The Yardbirds, the Small Faces and The Who, which he could really relate to. I hated the uniformity of punk but the mod revival was perfect for me. It was a tragedy when Sham 69 split because Dave Dee suddenly found that Pursey's dream was dropped from the label and all our contracts were consigned to the dustbin."

The Chords' experience with JP Productions served to confirm the general confusion and mistrust surrounding the music industry's relationship with the early mod revival. The now label-less Chords had recorded the first mod revival single, but they never got to release it. That prize went to their rivals, The Merton Parkas, whose label, Beggars Banquet, insisted that their weak and rather embarrassing paean to scooters, 'You Need Wheels', be their debut. The 45 came in a picture sleeve, with an embroidered 'parka patch' stapled to it and a photograph of the band perched on a couple of Lambrettas. The world at large was not impressed.

The Chords, however, were saved by the legendary BBC Radio 1 DJ and Undertones obsessive John Peel, who, uniquely among the broadcasting establishment, had proved receptive to the concept of a 'mod revival'. Peel saw the new scene as an obvious successor to punk because it was both younger and far more working class than the punk scene of a year or so earlier. He called The Chords in for a coveted 'Peel Session', which did the 'industry' trick; two months after the JP Productions deal had fallen through, A&R man Jim Cook re-signed The Chords to Polydor.

By the spring of 1979, the mod revival had arrived, and in a big way. But Purple Hearts guitarist Simon Stebbing remained suspicious of any mainstream media interest.

"I read one slag-off of Purple Hearts and it was actually great. It was really well written; some of the points they made were valid but it soon became apparent that the whole piece was actually bullshit. The journalist claimed that we all stood up there on stage with Rickenbackers; I mean, they clearly hadn't watched the gig. It was an easy mistake to make, as Weller played a Rickenbacker, so a lazy journalist could write a review without actually seeing the band, just adding some 'Rickenbacker flavour'. It made me laugh at first but after a while it made me angry. What right did they have to slag us off even though it was obvious they hadn't even been to the gig? That created a demand for objective reviews and, to be honest, after a while, the only objective reviews we were getting came from the growing fanzine scene."

BOB BRIXTON PRISON MARTEN

JUST JEFF SHADBOLT

few more of their dates:

SIMON STEBBING

GARY SPARKS....

Chords drummer Buddy Ascott felt the same: "The real importance of mod fanzines was in the first six months of the revival, before the industry hacks cottoned on to what was going on. There was a school of thought that once the *NME* and *Sounds* wrote about mod culture, it was already too late. The coolest mod I ever knew, a guy called Steve – seemed to have everything, a cool mod girlfriend and the first scooter I ever saw – he'd already walked away by June '79 because of the media interest. And he wasn't alone."

In spite of a warm reception from music journalist Garry Bushell, the 'McCulloch angle' was the one the majority of the established press followed. Comfortable staff journalists in their mid-to late thirties, who saw these preening, working-class upstarts as a threat to their beloved art punk and bands like Gang Of Four and The Mekons, who had swept all asunder as 1978 had turned into 1979, hated the mod revival with a passion.

In fact, by spring 1979 the mainstream media viewed the revival with the same mistrust they reserved for proper working-class boot-boy bands, like Angelic Upstarts and Cockney Rejects. With the exception of Bushell's work, reviews were, on the whole, disparaging, and within 12 months the word 'mod' was to become a millstone around the necks of the bands associated with the revival's early days.

But while the mainstream media largely ignored the burgeoning scene, the bands and their fans were growing at an exponential rate. In Buddy Ascott's words, "A vacuum is soon filled," and in February 1979, three intrepid would-be journalists stepped into the fray with the first truly great mod fanzine, *Maximum Speed*.

Maximum Speed – Goffa Gladding
Clive Reams and Kim Gault
London 1979.

№7 MAXIMUM SPECIAL • TOUR EDITION

SPEED

THE RISE AND RISE OF THE MODZINE

Maximum Speed – Goffa Gladding,
Clive Peams and Kim Gault,
London 1979.
Shake! – Dom Kenny and Mike,
London 1980.

Bill Brewster, DJ historian and co-author of *Last Night A DJ Saved My Life*, was a young mod revival punter who had just moved up to London from his home town Grimsby. "I first bought a mod fanzine either in or outside the Bridge House Hotel in Canning Town, sometime in 1979. It was *Maximum Speed*. Since the mod revival was either derided or ignored by the mainstream press, these inky samizdats became crucial centres of information and gossip for the whole scene and were as essential back then as an original pair of Sta-Prest trousers."

Co-editor Goffa Gladding remembers the very early days of the first modzine: "We started *Maximum Speed* in around January or February 1979 because we felt that our scene wasn't being properly represented by the likes of *Melody Maker*, *Sounds* and *NME*. It felt like we were right in the middle of something happening, something new and exciting, and that it would be quite good fun to write about it. The fanzine started off as something for a small group of people who all knew each other; it was full of in-jokes and reviews of gigs that we had all been to, which was why we began by making just 30 or 40 copies. It was essentially something that was stitched together, photocopied and stapled, and given away or flogged to people down the pub for less than 10 bob."

The editors and producers of the first mod revival fanzines touted their wares at such disparate venues as the Barge Aground in Barking, the Bridge House Hotel in Canning Town, the Wellington in Waterloo, the King's Head in Deptford, the Fulham Greyhound and occasionally at the grounds of their football teams of choice.

Maximum Speed may have been the first mod fanzine to hit the streets but it was soon joined by others.

Shake, edited by 15-year-old mod face Dominic Kenny, was one of the earliest zines. Brian Kotz, lead vocalist of the revival band Back To Zero, remembers Dom well.

"By the end of 1980, he published what I believe to be his last edition, co-edited by Mike 'The Psych' Jones [lead vocalist in The Playn Jayn and sometime manager of the mod/psych shop, the Regal*]. As well as featuring a mad cartoon story by Mike about a mod on an acid trip, it contained a hilarious interview with Shane MacGowan from The Nips. Astonishingly, a couple of years later Dom ended up in Kingston, Jamaica, recording a ragga album for the legendary reggae producer Prince Jammy, called *Ready For Dominick*. There was a small feature in one of the music rags at the time; he would still have been in his teens then. In around 2001, I was at a Long Tall Shorty gig at the Borderline and a gangly chap approached me, slightly pallid – he knew me, I was baffled... it was Dom! I had quite a long chat with him. When I mentioned [his former co-editor] Mike Jones, he became a bit emotional. Dom had evidently been in some trouble in his locality, and his friendship with Mike gave him direction to carry on with the fanzine, grow away from bad influences and go forward from there."

*The Regal was a men's clothes shop founded by designer Andrew Yiannakou and originally based in Kensington Market. Yiannakou's original late sixties paisley-style patterns became a mainstay and huge influence on the early psych scene.

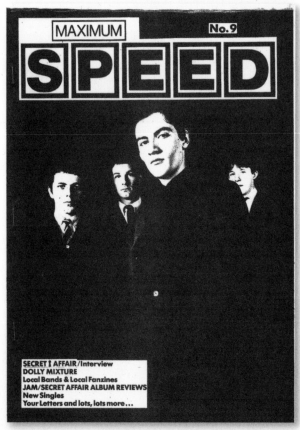

Maximum Speed — Goffa Gladding, Clive Reams
and Kim Gault, London 1979.

£1 MAXIMUM BackToNormal Issue

SPEED

Issue Nº 4

4/-

MUSIC
MACHINE
REVIEW
• • • • •

PURPLE
HEARTS

The Detours
• • • •

THE FIXATIONS
• • • •

Little Rockers

+

THE WHO IN
CANNES

PLUS

LETTERS, PIX
AND RESULTS

TRIAD
MAY 20

DIRECTION, REACTION, CREATION.

MERTON PARKAS

MP'S.SMALLHRS.NEWHEARTS.

direction direction direction direction direction
reaction reaction reaction reaction reaction
creation creation creation creation creation

Another very early and very professional fanzine was *Direction Reaction Creation*, or *DRC* for short, established in South-east London by Jon Obadiah.

Brian again: "Jon started *DRC* in '79, but I didn't really get to know him until 1980, which was the peak year for his zine. By then, I wasn't in Back To Zero but had formed a new band called Bees By Post, and he was an acquaintance of the drummer, Guy... and they were the first zine to write extensively about us, which was a big help. I remember driving past their local record shop, Cloakes in Streatham High Road, on my way to Brighton, and seeing the latest edition in the window with my photo on the cover – a surreal moment!

"Jon edited the fanzine with another guy, although he was the obvious talent when it came to writing. His work on The Chords was of value and, infamously, his article on psych music was cribbed almost word for word in places by Bob Manton for the Purple Hearts song 'Let's Get A Burger, Man' [also the title of the piece, which itself was taken from something *Shake*'s Dom had said to Jon at the height of the psych revival].

"The last edition of *DRC* was larger format, and Jon had had the wherewithal to arrange for the Long Tall Shorty flexi*, possibly the first such free gift from a modzine, but that was it. I think he may have gone on to write for the local press in South London for a while, but he's now off the radar, which is a shame."

Suddenly, modzines were everywhere. So just what was it that made them so important to the burgeoning scene?

Buddy Ascott: "Mod fanzines were vitally important in spreading the word about gigs and events, but, more importantly, they were like technical manuals, dispensing advice to countless would-be and proto-mods, eager to learn all they could about this new way of life!"

Simon Stebbing: "I wasn't too impressed with punk fanzines actually. I suppose the only one I read was *Sniffin' Glue*. As a band member, though, I remember being very flattered when Purple Hearts made it into *Maximum Speed.* I mean, we weren't in a band for the attention we could get; we all felt that didn't really matter because we were just happy and excited playing for our mates. The early mod-rock scene seemed like a pretty small club, an exclusive club that so very, very few people belonged to. When I first saw us mentioned in *Maximum Speed*, I felt it was really sincere because they weren't getting paid for it. It was our fanzine, exclusive to our world and that made the whole thing very interesting. It wasn't about some invented life that you weren't part of, it was about our world, what was happening to us, who was playing, and it reflected our way of life. As a band member you wanted to read up on other shows, you'd want to know about the competition."

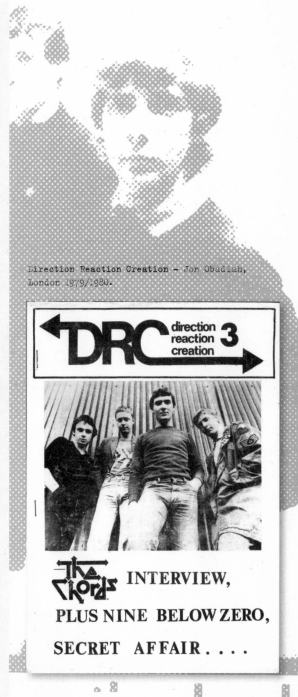

Direction Reaction Creation – Jon Obadiah, London 1979/1980.

* The flexi disc that Brian refers to is included with the deluxe edition of this very book.

direction reaction creation
direction reaction creation
direction reaction creation
direction reaction creation
direction reaction creation

the chords bureau
seb shelton
eight **moondogs regal** eight

direction reaction creation

long tall shorty flexi-disc...

direction reaction creation

DRC direction reaction creation **4**

THE CHORDS

THE MODS !

purple hearts

INTERVIEWS

PLUS THE JAM......

DRC direction reaction creation **5**

BEES
BY
POST

CHORDS LTS
PURPLE HEARTS+ MORE

DRC direction reaction creation **6**

LONG long tall shorty interview

Shorty

purple hearts chords psychedelia

direction direction direction direction direction
reaction reaction reaction reaction reaction
creation creation creation creation creation **7**

have you

the chords

heard the frog joke...

affair

speedball - long tall shorty - who .

Direction Reaction Creation
Jon Obadiah, London 1980/1981.

Paul Weller, whose soon-to-be iconic band the music press regularly disparaged early on, said: "I saw a lot of fanzines in the early punk days, I mean in '76 and '77. There was *Sniffin' Glue* from Mark Perry, *48 Thrills* from Adrian Thrills and Shane MacGowan's *Bondage*. I had never even thought about the possibility of doing your own little magazine until I saw them; I thought they were wonderful and written by people my own age, all of us 'waiting for something to happen'. They made the established music papers seem less important, too. The weekly press ultimately ended up taking in a lot of the upstart fanzine editors and writers and copying their style."

But while *48 Thrills* offered a way into the mainstream music press for its teenage editor, the same couldn't have been said for his mod equivalent, Goffa Gladding, a year or so later.

"I never really wanted to be a real journalist but this didn't seem to deter the people at *Sounds* magazine, who came along and asked me if I would write about mod stuff for them. They had obviously seen *Maximum Speed* and thought that I could contribute something. It started slowly, with a couple of mod revival pieces, but after a while they asked me to do a couple of reviews. Now, the problem was that they chose Iron Maiden and then The Fall. Neither of them were my cup of tea, but, thinking I might as well give it a go, I trekked up to the old Acklam Hall in Notting Hill to see Mark E. Smith and, rather unsurprisingly, I didn't enjoy it at all.

"See, *Sounds* was basically just like a great big fanzine and essentially people bought it to read about the bands they liked, so you couldn't really comment on things too negatively. It wasn't like *Melody Maker* or the *New Musical Express* would have been. So when they asked me to write about stuff I wasn't necessarily interested in and I reviewed it genuinely or rather from a critical perspective, by and large they didn't publish it. To be honest, I found it difficult to get out of bed and write positively about Iron Maiden. And that was when my broader journalistic career fell flat on its face…"

Conversely, Chris Hunt, editor of the early eighties modzine *Shadows And Reflections*, saw his fanzine as a route into the world of 'real' journalism.

"I'd always wanted to be a magazine editor, but really my ambition was to create a fanzine that I could turn into my own national magazine – just like Tony Fletcher had achieved with *Jamming!*. Unfortunately that wasn't to be, but my fanzine's quality encouraged a small publishing company to offer me a job editing their one-shot magazines. Ironically, the first national magazine I was asked to launch was a one-off heavy metal magazine called *Solid Rock*. When they offered me the job, I said, 'As a mod, it's my ultimate ambition to be the editor of a heavy metal magazine.' The joke was missed but that opportunity launched a 30-year career as a magazine and book editor."

Its a Legal Matter Baby, A Mod Guide to Sex —
Eddie Piller and Terry Rawlings 1984.
Direction Reaction Creation
Jon Obadiah, London 1980.
Shadows And Reflections — Chris Hunt
Ely, Cambridgeshire 1982.

But how did the artists themselves feel about fanzines? Paul Weller often went out on a limb to help the editors secure review copies and guest lists for Jam releases and tours. He appeared in all the major mod fanzines, often giving extensive interviews that were much more detailed than many appearing in the mainstream press.

"I always thought that it was as, if not more, important to speak to the fanzines as it was to the 'trades'. Fanzines didn't have the same agenda as the *Melody Maker* and the *NME*… they only really wrote about the people they liked, the questions were more interesting and [they covered] what the fans wanted to hear about."

Manchester's first and finest punk group Buzzcocks were another punk band who wore their mod influences on their sleeves.

Guitarist Steve Diggle: "I always thought that fanzines were extremely important. Being interviewed by somebody that had a deep passion for what you did and asked you very direct questions, the kind of questions that rock journalists wouldn't even have thought about… that was where you learned what was really going on out in the audience. It wasn't edited or controlled by corporate magazines and consequently it was a sometimes brutal, sometimes beautiful reality…"

The fanzines assumed ever-greater importance when general indifference towards mod bands in the mainstream music press soon turned into an all-out backlash that threatened to harm their careers.

Goffa Gladding apportions part of the blame to *Maximum Speed*. "I guess we should take some of the responsibility for the backlash with our overuse of the bloody mod tag. In all honesty, the Hearts, The Chords and Secret Affair would have stood very happily on their own within the post-new wave type thing without any help from us! When you look at the quality of the music it really does stand up on its own without needing the mod tag."

But Gary Sparks of Purple Hearts disagrees: "I'm not so sure that we would have been noticed. There were so many great bands out there that it felt good to be a part of something that was distinctly different from punk. Something we could call our own and actually be a part of, and that was why *Maximum Speed* was so important."

Jamming!'s Tony Fletcher*, another early fanzine editor with mod leanings, was quick to notice the mod revival washing around the late punk scene. "There were always hints of the mod revival around the music that I was already into. I was a massive Jam fan from 1977, so was quite used to seeing suits and parkas at their shows. And there were always bands that leaned towards the music somewhat – Generation X with 'Ready Steady Go' being a prime example. But in early 1979, it just suddenly happened. Almost overnight it seemed like there was a scene at the Wellington in

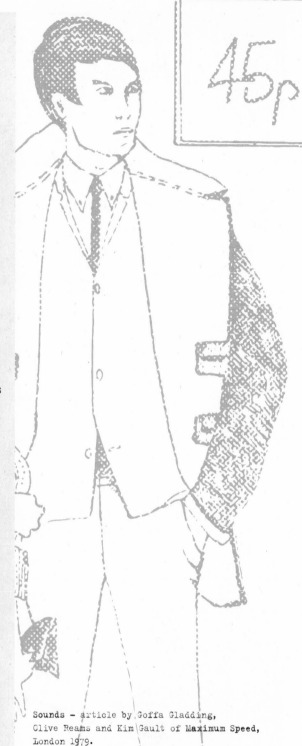

Sounds – article by Goffa Gladding, Clive Reams and Kim Gault of Maximum Speed, London 1979.

*Tony Fletcher would eventually go on to work in the mainstream press, even appearing as an interviewer on Channel 4's music show *The Tube*, which ran from 1982 to 1987. Later he became a best-selling author of rock biographies. His *Dear Boy: The Life of Keith Moon* is regarded as the definitive work on The Who's legendary drummer, while his autobiography, *Boy About Town*, is based on his early life and career as a fanzine editor.

WHO's WHO

By Kim Gaunt, Clive and Goffa
Gladding of Maximum Speed
mod fanzine

Clive, Kim and Goffa of Maximum Speed.

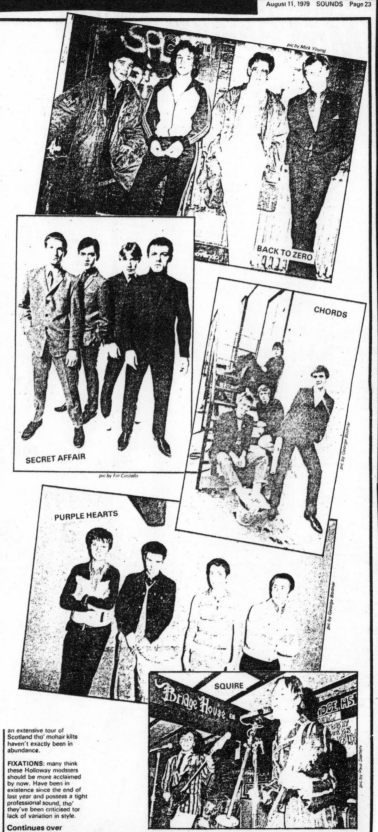

pic by Mick Young

BACK TO ZERO

SECRET AFFAIR

pic by Fin Castello

CHORDS

pic by George Bodnar

PURPLE HEARTS

pic by George Bodnar

SQUIRE

pic by Paul Slattery

BACK TO ZERO: the band generally regarded to be 'the next big one after' the Hearts/Chords/Affair/Merton Parkas. Formed in the Enfield /Southgate areas of N. London at the beginning of the year, their catchy, melodic yet moody songs have gained them a loyal following round London and the Home Counties. First single on Chris Parry's Fiction label will be 'Back To Back'/'New Side Of Heaven', both written by guitarist Sam Burnett.'

CHORDS: First band to play the now defunct Wellington, Waterloo; wasted a couple of months being protegees of the Hersham Horror and are now back on the right track with Polydor. Have been receiving unwarranted 'in-crowd' verbal from those who know no better but vinyl success guaranteed.

KILLERMETERS: The mod band in the north. They have a single out on Psycho records 'Why Should It Happen To Me' which is excellent. Their one major venture from Yorkshire to London was as support to the Chords at the Marquee in June, which didn't really work out.

MERTON PARKAS: we're sitting on the fence for this one. Loved by some, loathed my millions largely owing to the *Sun* article etc. etc. Somewhat wimpy single, 'You Need Wheels' already in the chart, album due shortly. Dismissed by hardcore London mods as cabaret-playing bandwagon-jumpers but strong teen-market potential.

MODS: The most improved band on the scene, once played almost all covers but now have some of the best originals around. High spot probably was supporting the Undertones at Cambridge, and they're now beginning to headline many venues. They were one of the first and now at last they're one of the best.

PURPLE HEARTS: Another E. London/Essex band. First Mods to get any music press coverage (by some twat name of Bushell) and undoubtably in the top four. Their first single 'Millions Like Us' b/w 'Beat That' and the 'March Of The Mods' tour will consolidate their position in Division One.

SECRET AFFAIR: Formed from the ashes of three no-hope bands (no disrespect intended lads) into the future world-dominating S.A. Massive vinyl potential with about six guaranteed chart songs in their set and electric stage presence. The ones most likely to succeed. Will fully justify both recent press overkill and silly record company advances being offered. First single, 'Time For Action'/'Soho Strut' due out on Arista soon.

SQUIRE: 3 months ago they were working hard getting nowhere in Surrey, now they're a ubiquitous sight on the London scene. Supported everyone worthwhile and altho' they don't have a following they're highly respected as being v. melodic. Are linked with Twist 'n' Shout records and have a single 'B.A.B.Y' out in August. Lightweight sound but stand out as having a big future.

TEENBEATS: Currently the hip Mod band to say you like and why not indeed. From the 'rockers stronghold' of Hastings they play energetic, exciting pop. Their excellent cover of 'I Can't Control Myself' is already on release on Safari records and the 5-piece combo are now under the expert guidance of Jerry 'Skinny' Floyd.

BEGGAR: originally from S.Wales, now based in Leyton, E. London. Play raw-edged Merseybeat style R&B. Of their tracks on the Bridge House 'Mods May Day' album, 'Broadway Show' would be a great single. Have just completed an extensive tour of Scotland tho' mohair kilts haven't exactly been in abundance.

FIXATIONS: many think these Holloway modsters should be more acclaimed by now. Have been in existence since the end of last year and possess a tight professional sound, tho' they've been criticised for lack of variation in style.

Continues over

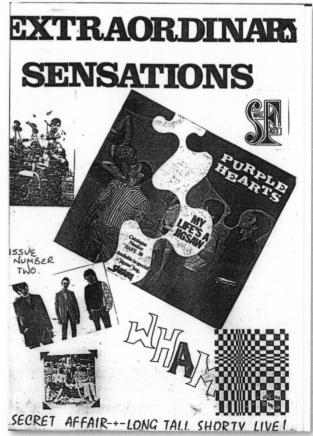

Extraordinary Sensations
Eddie Piller and Terry
Rawlings, Essex 1981/1982.

INTERVIEWS WITH;

SMALL WORLD
ROB MANTON PART 2
LONG TALL SHORTY

PLUS ARTICLES
ON;

REACTIONS,

THE JAM,

CLUBS,

FANZINES,

**RHYTHM
+ SOUL,**

1981,

THE PILOTS,

**GEORGIE
FAME.**

+ MORE !!

ISSUE NUMBER 6

EXTRAORDINARY SENSATIONS

30P

Patriotic – Ray Margetson, London 1981.
Get Up and Go – Tony Lordan and
Vaughn Toulouse, London 1979.
Roadrunner – Steve Whiffen, Kent 1980/1981.

Waterloo, not far from my school, and that there were a number of fully functioning bands, and that *Quadrophenia* was about to be released, and that television shows were already jumping on it and the major labels, too, and suddenly people at my school were wearing parkas over their uniforms – in summer!"

Although *Jamming!* was seen more or less as a punk fanzine, Tony's obsession with The Jam meant that there was substantial crossover with the burgeoning mod revival. Therefore, it was among the last of the mainstream punk (or, rather, what would now be called 'indie') fanzines that would eventually mix both the punk and mod genres. However, in spite of mod's similarities to punk, the adherents were starting to put clear blue water between themselves and their punk forebears.

Tony Lordan, who ran **Get Up And Go!** with his best mate and partner Vaughn Toulouse, thought that the split was ideologically driven. The pair had originally established their mod fanzine as a way of promoting their mod/ska hybrid band Guns For Hire, but the concept of a new mod fanzine soon caught on.

"While **Maximum Speed** was clearly the early mover and shaker on the scene, we also had **Direction Reaction Creation** and **Shake**, both edited by keen young mods and both adding something to the narrative. With **Get Up And Go!** we thought we could add to the growing network of fanzines. You got a certain amount of power within the scene as editor of a fanzine that sold a reasonable number of copies. We might have started **Get Up And Go!** as a way of promoting our band, but by the time we came up with our second issue, we genuinely had a following."

Goffa Gladding again: "For a long time we were the only magazine in town. I don't really remember any others until later. For the time that we did it, we were literally it. [However,] **Get Up And Go!** came pretty early and they were extremely helpful to **Maximum Speed**. Tony went running round London putting our posters up for us... Later, **Shake**, **Direction Reaction Creation**, **Patriotic**, **Roadrunner** and **Extraordinary Sensations** came to the fore as we were running down or had already stopped."

And it was this second wave of revival fanzines that really inspired the next generation of mod fanzine editors, including myself: "I had been a big fan of **Maximum Speed**, which I first picked up outside the North Bank at the Boleyn Ground, Upton Park. West Ham had a big mod following in early '79, with the likes of Grant Fleming and The Glory Boys who followed Secret Affair, but I had realised that towards the second half of the year, the editors of the fanzine were getting bored. The gap between issues was getting longer, and while the fanzines themselves were becoming more professional in layout, the content was becoming detached from the fanbase and less interested in our scene.

EXTRAORDINARY SENSATIONS NO 13

EXTRAORDINARY SENSATIONS

No 7　　　　　**30P**

PARIS

 SQUIRE　

Long Tall Shorty
making time

MARTHA & THE VANDELLAS

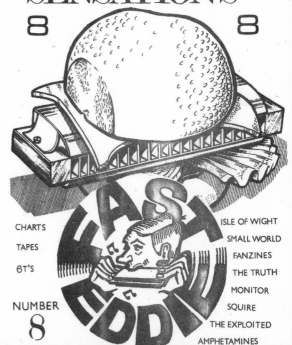

EXTRAORDINARY SENSATIONS

8　　　**8**

FAST EDDIE

CHARTS
TAPES
6T'S

NUMBER
8

ISLE OF WIGHT
SMALL WORLD
FANZINES
THE TRUTH
MONITOR
SQUIRE
THE EXPLOITED
AMPHETAMINES

EXTRAORDINARY

SENSATIONS **12**

THE JOURNAL FOR DISCERNING STYLISTS EVERYWHERE!

Extraordinary Sensations
Eddie Piller and Terry
Rawlings, Essex 1982/1984.

"I had met the editors of **Get Up And Go!** at a Small Hours gig at the Rock Garden in mid-'79. It was a tiny venue but full of people who all knew each other. I loved the band and was totally convinced by the fanzine. Tony Lordan and Vaughn Toulouse literally took me under their wing and taught me how to go about producing a mod fanzine."

While the other fanzines were getting off the ground, Goffa and the rest of the editorial team at **Maximum Speed** were losing momentum.

"We got to Issue 10. I mean number 9 had sold literally 9,000 copies, but in the end we just lost interest. I suppose I carried on taking subscriptions and advance payments for Issue 10 but, to be honest, we just couldn't face it. I kidded myself that we would eventually roll out Issue 10 but in the end we didn't. I suppose we invented crowd funding! Send me your subscription and I will (well may, but probably not) send your copy in the post. It wasn't that I didn't want to, it was because the whole thing had become a bind. We just walked away."

Despite the loss of mod's earliest fanzine, throughout the summer of 1979, the mod scene continued to grow, as more young kids joined the revival.

But there was now competition: 2 Tone, which fused ska with punk rock attitude, and for the previous six months had been seen as a minor offshoot of the mod revival, started to come to the fore. Bands like The Special AKA (who would become The Specials), Madness and later The Beat and The Selecter began appearing on revival bills at the Electric Ballroom and the Lyceum, often as headliners. Even Dexy's Midnight Runners went from fourth on the bill to Purple Hearts to headlining the same venue soon after.

And then it happened. On August 16th, 1979, that film was released.

Roadrunner — Steve Whiffen, Kent 1980/1981.
Patriotic — Ray Margetson, London 1981.

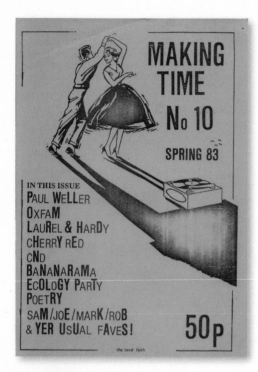

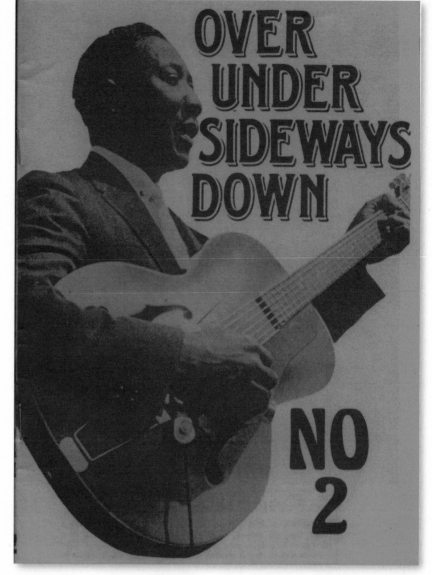

Making Time - Joe, Mark, Sam and Robin,
Herne Bay 1983.
Over Under Sideways Down.
The New Stylist - R Paddison, Leeds 1983.
Odd Issue - John Davies, Barry, Wales 1984.

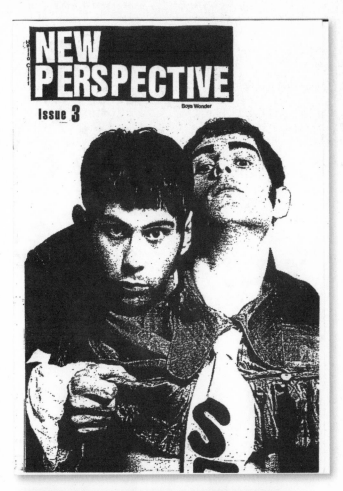

Wow + VAT! – David Montgomery (RIP), Northampton 1990/1991.
New Perspective – Rodders, Cambridge 1992.
Modern Breakdown – mid 80's.
Get Happy – Pierre Naggar, Rome, Italy 1991.

'MILLIONS LIKE US':

MOD GOES MAINSTREAM

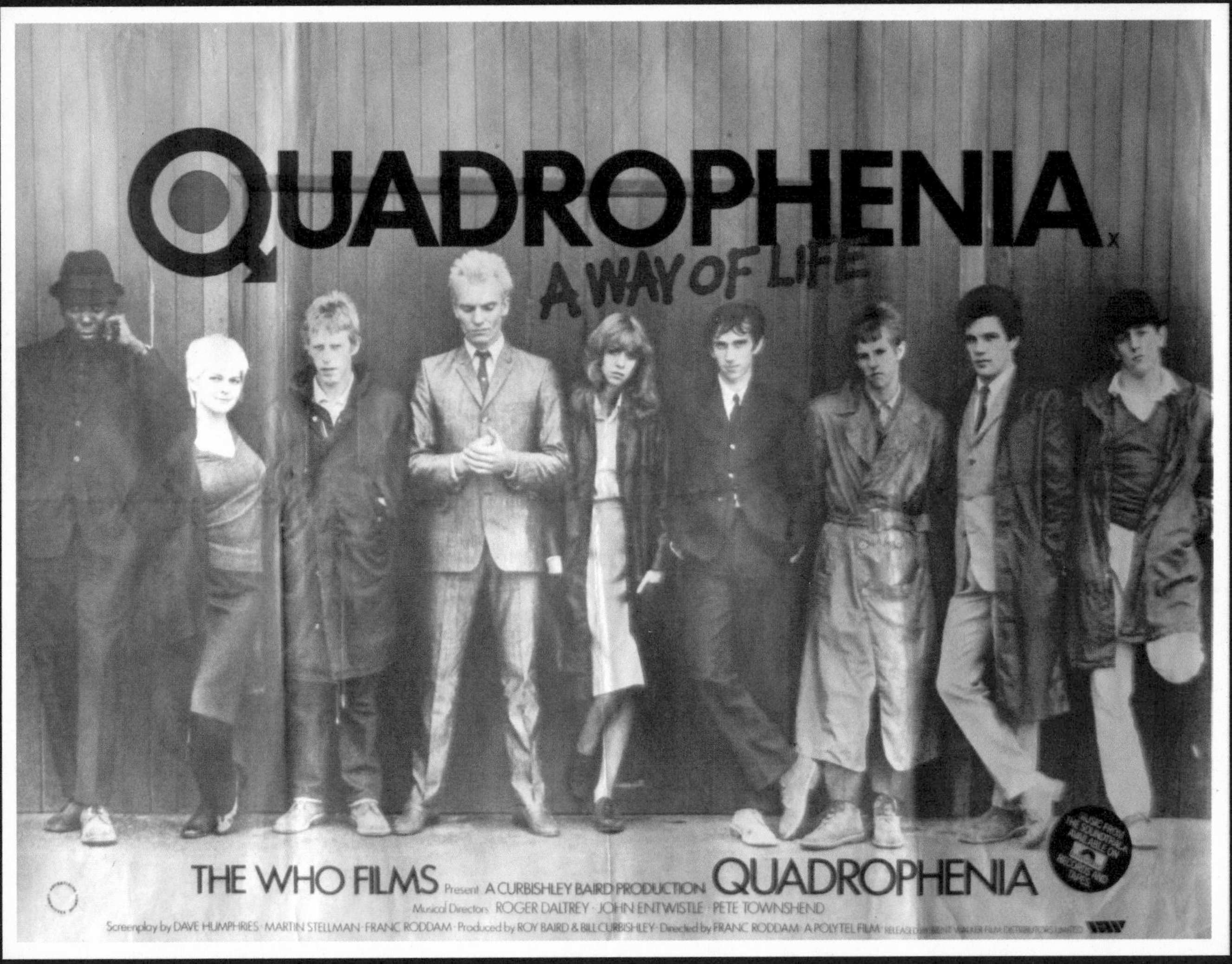

QUADROPHENIA x
A WAY OF LIFE
THE WHO FILMS Present A CURBISHLEY BAIRD PRODUCTION QUADROPHENIA
Musical Directors ROGER DALTREY · JOHN ENTWISTLE · PETE TOWNSHEND
Screenplay by DAVE HUMPHRIES · MARTIN STELLMAN · FRANC RODDAM · Produced by ROY BAIRD & BILL CURBISHLEY · Directed by FRANC RODDAM · A POLYTEL FILM

While many of the mod revival's originators saw *Quadrophenia* as the final nail in the coffin, it was probably the biggest boost ever to hit the scene.

In June of that year, The Who had released the pioneering rock documentary *The Kids Are Alright* to general indifference in cinemas across the country. While young mods may not have flocked to that particular banner (The Who had a much longer period as proper long-haired heavy rockers than they ever did as a mod band), the film at least gave kids like us a chance to meet like-minded travellers along the mod path. The revival was still in its infancy but the realisation that other people were focused on a life following The Jam, Secret Affair or the enormous number of emerging young mod bands actually brought the scene and its followers closer together.

I recall: "We went to the opening night of *The Kids Are Alright* at the ABC cinema in South Woodford. There were four of us from school, but we were absolutely gobsmacked to see a whole gang of other young mods in the queue. It turned out that they were from Epping, Hainault, Buckhurst Hill and Chingford. That night gave us a load of instant mates and from that point on we all went to gigs in town together."

Following the release of *Quadrophenia*, the mod revival suffered something of a crisis of confidence. Members of the music industry suddenly scrambled to sign their own particular 'mod band', and while Polydor and their Fiction imprint had been quick off the mark, the other major labels – and most of the indie labels – were soon getting in on the act.

This plethora of new bands signing to record labels created another wave of interest in the mainstream music press, which resulted in yet more young adherents and inspired more fanzine editors. Late 1979 was surely the golden period for the original mod revival and within a year, fanzines were appearing nationally and in their hundreds.

And, in spite of the fact that, in retrospect, people tend to view the mod revival as a 'boy thing', girls ran many of the fanzines. Not that this seemed remarkable at the time – it was just a mod thing!

Brian Kotz remembers **Own Up Time**, which was founded by Tina Skinner of the Wembley Girls (now a senior marketing manager at Parlophone Records) and was probably the first modzine with a female editor.

"The front cover of the first issue was striking. It was made up from the pattern of a 1960s paisley shirt. People forget now how iconic the paisley pattern was to the mod scene; Weller wore a paisley shirt on the cover for the single 'When You're Young', and they were almost impossible to find in shops. Psych was kicking in as an influence, and apart from the occasional paisley shirt in Flip, the vintage shop in Covent Garden, you just couldn't get them until the Regal came on the scene. The other thing about **Own Up**

Page from issue 6 of **Maximum Speed**
Goffa Gladding, Clive Reams and
Kim Gault, London 1979.

The Kids Are Alright

Okay - so I know that the '79 Who have got about as much in common with '79 Mods as I have with Andy Williams, but what we have here is a funny and always entertaining history of a band that's always been one of the undisputed leaders in the world of rock 'n' roll, whether it be by smashing guitars or driving cars into swimming pools or by being banned for wearing a jacket made from a Union Jack. So why the review if the Who are just another name on a lapel badge? Because the 'Orrible '00 have got more to say about what's happening to-day in five minutes of archive screen time than half the bands currently treading the (already worn) Mod circuit. The buzz that you get, even sitting in a cinema, when Townshend chops out the staccato opening chords to 'Can't Explain' or the feed-back in 'Anyway, Anyhow, Anywhere' is something that you'll have to experience for yourself - for me, anyway, it's a feeling that I get from no other live band.
Still, back to the film. I think a lot of you will have seen it by now, or

will have read reviews in the music press, so you will know that it's a documentary charting the career of The Who from playing in sweaty boozers in West London as the High Numbers, thru Woodstock, to the (near) present with a specially staged gig at Shepperton. There's lots of live concert footage plus various interview segments (most of which are genuinely hilarious) and T.V. show spots, including some memorable 'Ready, Steady, Go' clips.

Double Breasted — Sharon Wood and Jennie
Baillie, Perth, Scotland 2009.
Go Go — Jackie Topham and Bernadine Wood,
Dagenham, Essex 1985.
Uptight — Tracy Scanlan and Mandy Wadey,
Essex 1980.
The Way Ahead — Janet Page, Swindon 1983.

Time is that it featured a great mix of old and new – you would get a piece about The Troggs or The Move next to an article on one of the new bands. A great read."

The Way Ahead was another female-led mid-eighties zine. Janet Page, now a creative artworker, was based in Swindon. "I sold it mainly in Carnaby Street but also by mail order and at gigs. We regularly had events in Swindon and although I did most of the work myself, I had contributions from the photographer Darren Russell and Mark Everden did some of the music articles. I only made four issues and then let it die a quiet death…"

Tracy Scanlan had started a fanzine called *Uptight!* with her friend Mandy Wadey while they were still at high school in Chigwell, Essex, back in 1980.

"I think we'd seen other fanzines being passed around at school and decided we wanted to give it a go ourselves because it seemed like a fun thing to do! It was a bit of a challenge getting it copied and stuff and that's why we eventually knocked it on the head – it would be a lot different these days, with all the technology available. I don't think we did too bad for a couple of 15-year-old amateurs!"

As recently as 2011, Jennie Baillie from Perth in Scotland was running the superbly crafted *Double Breasted*, which garnered national distribution. Originally established with Sharon Wood from Glasgow and then continued by Jennie alone, it was proof that the gender of a fanzine's editor was, in most cases, absolutely irrelevant.

GoGo's Bernadine Wood felt the same: "Was it different for girls? I don't think that was really a factor for us. Yes, the scene was mostly male orientated, but we didn't set out to make a female fanzine. We just wanted to do something that captured everything that was going on – all the different bands, music, art, theatre, the sixties – and most of all we really enjoyed doing it."

In the end, what mattered was the connection to the fans. Kev Bagnall, editor of *XL5*, sums up why he felt there was such a need for modzines.

"Primarily because, after the initial rush from *Sounds*, national coverage died – and there was so much more to [the scene] than parkas, scooters and tribalism. It wasn't until later that I discovered there was already a massive scene up north, and certainly outside of London – but that may well be indicative of the London scene itself, which was very insular. I lived in central London, and very rarely made it beyond the borders of the yet-to-be-built M25, even though a lot of my friends and contemporaries, such as Steve 'Roadrunner' Whiffen [editor of the hugely important and successful *Roadrunner* fanzine and usually referred to as Steve Roadrunner] and Eddie Piller, lived out there. Fanzines were an important part of not only keeping the scene going but also informing readers of new bands to look out for and go and see."

THE WAY AHEAD

no.2

P.L.Page.

The Way Ahead
Janet Page, Swindon 1983/1984.

By 1982, the landscape had changed somewhat and the next generation of fanzines had come to the fore. They were no doubt helped by the fact that a small shop at the top of a spiral staircase in an arcade called the Rockafella Centre in Foubert's Place (behind Boots) in Carnaby Street had become a dedicated mod shop. While Carnaby Cavern (opposite the pub the Shakespeare's Head, which dates back to 1735) concentrated on suits and trousers, Robot, as it was then called, became a veritable Aladdin's cave of independently produced, mod-related items, from T-shirts and Harrington jackets to records and, most importantly, fanzines.

The shop was run (or actually, curated would be a better description) by the legendary Jimmy, who was originally from Singapore. While Jimmy never claimed to be a mod himself, Robot became a go-to destination for any mod visiting London for the day. It was crammed full with dozens of the latest fanzines, which were all stocked on 'sale or return', alongside parkas, monkey boots, badges and patches.

Now known somewhat laughably as the Carnaby Quarter (the area had yet to undergo any of its 1990s makeovers), Carnaby Street and the surrounding alleys and back roads were at the time an uninspiring, grubby mecca for 'visit London' tourist-tat emporiums and clapped-out fashion shops. But the last vestiges of Carnaby's legendary mod status, hard earned by the original menswear genius John Stephen and his ilk in the 1960s, had seeped into the nation's psyche, and so the street became the place for mods to see and be seen.

However, the early eighties was an especially dangerous time for young mod visitors to Carnaby Street; the skinhead wars were at their height and the street and its environs would invariably see trouble played out on a Saturday afternoon. Where young mods went, skinheads often prowled, demanding the obligatory 10 pence from unsuspecting teens, and their chosen point of ambush was at the top of the stairs outside Jimmy's shop.

For young mods, it could be a difficult and sometimes painful task acquiring the most recent fanzines. There was a 15-yard gap between the top of the stairs and the large glass doors of Robot, and while the skinheads would never dare to enter Jimmy's kingdom, his young shoppers often had to run the gauntlet of kicks, punches and spit from the glue-sniffing skins who congregated there. The police were often called and violence was near constant.

As the decade progressed, the skinhead presence declined. However, Robot faced a threat of a different kind. There was already a successful vintage clothes shop of the same name on the Kings Road in Chelsea and its owners objected to Robot's use of their trademarked name. The owner of the Carnaby Street version, Javid Alavi, and his manager Jimmy renamed their shop Merc and, faced with the threat of redevelopment of the internal mall at Foubert's Place, eventually relocated to Ganton Street.

Fightback – Rudi Adam, London 1981.
Page from issue 7 of Extraordinary
Sensations, Eddie Piller and Terry Rawlings,
Essex 1981/1982.

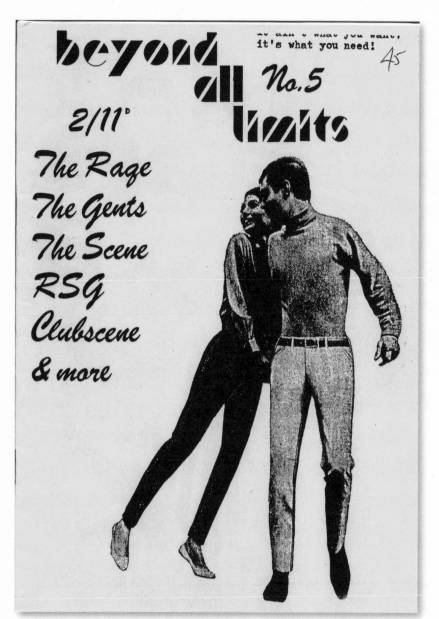

beyond all limits No.5

2/11ᵈ

...it's what you want,
it's what you need! 45

The Rage
The Gents
The Scene
RSG
Clubscene
& more

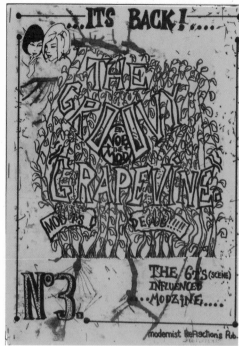

...ITS BACK!....

THE GROOVY GRAPEVINE

Nᵒ3.

THE 6T'S (SCENE)
INFLUENCED
...MODZINE!....

modernist Reflections Pub.

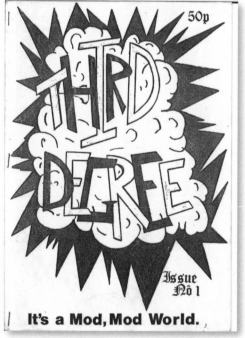

50p

THIRD DEGREE

Issue Nô1

It's a Mod, Mod World.

beyond all limits No.6

45.
THE HIGH STANDARD
NUMBER TWO   MODZINE

Beyond All Limits — Bell, Sheffield 1985.
The Groovy Grapevine — Nob, Northampton 1985.
Third Degree — Peter Mathieson, Aberdeen 1985.
The High Standard — Scarborough 1985.

The Café Society – Sheila, Liverpool. 1983.
Blind Badger – Dexy, Antrim 1991.
Absolute Beginners – Rob Cox, Exeter 1989.
Empty Dream – Neil Marsh, Kent 1981.
Watcha Gonna Do About It – Rob Messer, Essex1984.
Northern Survivor – R Paddison, Leeds 1982.

Patriotic — Ray Margetson, London
1981/1983.
Fabulous — Des Mannay, Cardiff 1984.
1 Way World — Paul Macnamara, Chris
Whaley and David Owens, Cardiff 1984.

If Merc became the focus of the mid-eighties mod revival in Carnaby Street, it also became the centre of fanzine sales, and at any one time you could find over 50 different titles in stock.

Ray Margetson, editor of **Patriotic**, recalls: "It was brilliant, actually. I could just drop off 50 copies of the latest issue, go back a week later and Jimmy would have sold them all and had the money waiting for me in an envelope. It was fantastic exposure, as he always had big window displays, which helped to increase **Patriotic**'s circulation enormously. Merc was important but also Sherry's and Terry Stokes' Right Track Records were big supporters. All of those took adverts in the magazine, which helped towards production costs. I think we were one of the first mod fanzines to approach advertisers as a business model."

GoGo's Bernadine Wood remembers how important Merc was in such a competitive market: "We distributed our fanzine mostly at gigs, but also got copies into a few shops, like the Merc in Carnaby Street, Sweet Charity in Kensington Market and Rock On Records in Camden Town. We made it to number one in the fanzine chart in Merc's shop window, which proved to be a massive boost to both profile and sales."

But it wasn't just Merc in London. Increasingly, independent outlets were popping up across the country and stocking the latest fanzine offerings. South Wales had an enormous teen mod scene, largely based in Newport, Swansea and Cardiff but extending out to smaller outposts in the valleys. Spillers Records in Cardiff – which, founded in 1894, is the world's oldest record shop – soon became the largest stockist of fanzines outside London.

Paul Macnamara, who edited the Welsh zine **1 Way World!** for four issues from 1984 onwards along with Chris Whaley and David Owens, recalls: "We used to print 500 copies of each issue and get them stocked in Spillers. We used to sell the rest at places like the New Morning Club, the CCI Rallies and even at those brilliant mod all-dayers at the Ilford Palais. We could also check out what other people were up to by looking in Spillers."

Des Mannay, another Cardiff-based editor who compiled a couple of editions of his own zine, **Fabulous!** in 1984, continues: "While I was based in Cardiff I sold most copies of my fanzine in London, where I seemed to spend most of my time while not working (to raise money to travel to London!). **Fabulous!** was memorable for still using pounds, shillings and pence for the cover price rather than that new-fangled decimal coinage, as I was totally obsessed with the sixties at the time! I was also the first person to interview [the band] Makin' Time… I travelled up to Wolverhampton to interview them while taking a break from work with exhaustion. My doctor had given me these pills and told me not to drink under any circumstances! There lies another story….

PATRIOTIC

ISSUE 3

.... THE MODZINE IN TOUCH WITH MUSIC FROM THE STREETS ....

POW!

ZAP!

THE RETURN OF BATMOD!

MODS IN
HOLLAND +
AUSTRALIA

featuring:

CHORD'S
+DISTANT ECHO
INTERVIEWS

ONLOOKERS
007
VARIATIONS
DOLLY MIXTURE

(ABSOLUTELY NOTHING
ON THE PURPLE HEARTS!)

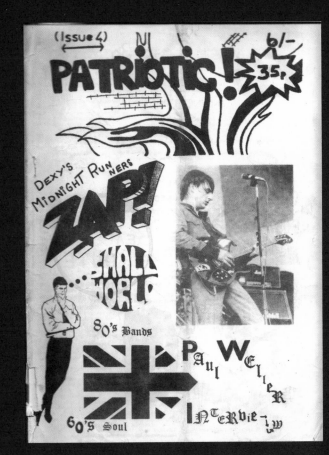

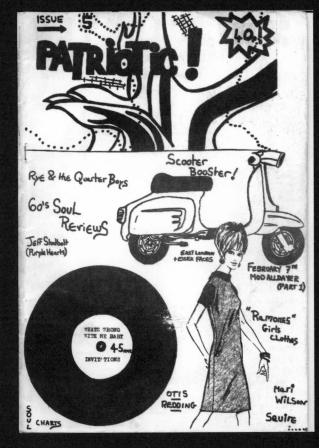

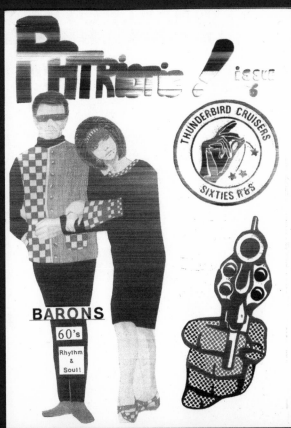

Patriotic – Ray Margetson
London 1981/1983.

"*Fabulous!* was also the cause of a fight between Mark Johnson of *The Phoenix List** and [singer and mod girl] Eleanor Rigby's manager Russell [Brennan] It was the start of a feud that lasted until they both disappeared from the scene… happy days!"

If, as the eighties progressed, the number of fanzines available increased dramatically, the reasons for starting them were exactly the same as they had been back in 1979.

Karl Bedingfield created the Cambridge-based *Shadows And Reflections* with his good friend Chris Hunt and it went on to become one of the most successful zines from that period.

"To be honest, I didn't really have the same commitment as Chris and dropped out after three issues. We were the first to champion a new local band called The Moment, who went on to greater things. They even named a song after me; it was called 'Karl's New Haircut'!"

Partner Chris is now a successful author, journalist and former commercial magazine editor.

"I was inspired to publish a mod fanzine through my disillusionment with the national music press and the lack of coverage given to the release of Secret Affair's third album, *Business As Usual,* a year earlier. The album was largely panned or ignored and I decided that I wanted to create a platform for writing about the music I loved, which was mainly mod or, more broadly, sixties-influenced pop.

"It took me a year to get around to doing something about it, but a chance meeting with Anthony Meynell of the band Squire in Carnaby Street prompted me to do an on-the-spot interview and gave me my first article. The mod scene at the time desperately needed the fanzine network because so much good music was being made but the mainstream music press was largely ignoring it."

In the winter of 1982, Paul Weller announced that The Jam were splitting. Many assumed that it signalled the end of the mod revival, but it proved to be anything but.

Chris Hunt again: "There were a lot of kids who were enthused by the 1979 mod revival but who weren't quite ready to move on to something new, whatever the mainstream music press told them. These kids formed the bands, started the fanzines, and filled the audiences for the second mod revival. We created our own self-contained little universe where we could exist in relative isolation. It helped that so much good music was being made at the time, but the fact that a lot of it was ignored outside of our world created a 'them against us' mentality that inspired quite an incredible sense of loyalty to the bands and the music.

*Johnson edited *The Phoenix List*, a weekly newsletter that featured news stories and, most importantly, gig and club listings pertinent to the scene… but more on Mark later in the book…

SHADOWS AND
REFLECTIONS

NO.1

squire
SCARLET PARTY
THE truth
SMALL WORLD
mari wilson

THE circles
THE Action

45 PencE

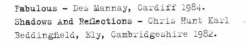
Fabulous – Des Mannay, Cardiff 1984.
Shadows And Reflections – Chris Hunt Karl
Beddingfield, Ely, Cambridgeshire 1982.

Shadows And Reflections - Chris Hunt
Ely, Cambridgeshire 1982/1986.

SHADOWS AND

REFLECTIONS

AND A GROOVY TIME WAS HAD BY ALL!

NO. 4

50p

SMALL WORLD

THE MOMENT

DEE WALKER

MAKIN' TIME

THE TIMES

THE BLADES

PLAYN JAYN

SURFIN' LUNGS

"I started **Shadows And Reflections** in the spring of 1983 and made a rather modest 175 copies, all of which sold. It took four months before Issue 2 was ready and I managed to sell 750 of those. By Christmas '83 I rushed out 1,200 copies of number 3 and I felt that the fanzine had its own look and feel. By Issue 6 (the final edition), we were regularly selling 2,000 copies."

Chris Hunt's experience is fairly typical for a fanzine editor. Inspired to make a difference (at whatever level, be it nationally or just to friends down the pub), the excitement and sense of achievement that comes with completing an issue and then seeing your efforts for sale and then someone actually reading it is a highly motivating factor.

Bernadine Wood and Jackie Topham's **GoGo** lasted 14 issues. "In the early days of the revival, the mod scene was extraordinarily vibrant with loads going on, and you could go to a different gig or a club most nights of the week. In the early to mid-eighties there was something of a lull and a lot of people dropped out of the scene or got into other kinds of music. When things suddenly started picking up, it was difficult to find out what was going on gig or club-wise, so we started **GoGo** with the intention of being a monthly informative fanzine. There were some other good fanzines around – the ones that stick out in my mind were **Shadows & Reflections**, **Extraordinary Sensations** and **In The Crowd**, as well as numerous one-off publications."

Stewart Hardman's **Have A Good Time** was the perfect example of a fanzine that was hugely significant to the local market, in this case Barnsley, Rotherham and Doncaster. Up to that point, **Northern Mod Scene**, edited by the prolific and scooter-riding Martin Dixon, was the biggest northern fanzine, but Stewart was perfectly placed to spread the word in his region.

He remembers: "I published seven issues between '84 and '89 and sold around 200 copies a time. The first issues were true-type written (before the days of computers) and I used double-sided sticky tape and then Pritt Stick to create the layout, which I would then photocopy. One batch would in turn pay for the next when I sold them. From Issue 3, I was in full-time employment and had access to a PC and word processor, which improved the final copy no end, but I still kept the same photocopy of the original sheets – this was before the days of laser printers, and I couldn't risk too much photocopying at work in a new job!

"I sold it at gigs and rallies up and down the country, and started receiving postal requests after getting reviews in other zines at the time – it went all over the world at times, which I was very humbled by. I also met loads of new 'scene-related' friends for the first time, and these friendships still exist today, some on a regular chat basis even now, and some led to me being invited to events and rallies abroad and discovering the local mod scenes, and in turn befriending a good deal of the people involved in them. Fantastic and exciting times, a great learning curve.

HAVE A GOOD TIME

MODZINE

ISSUE 5   35p

Have A Good Time – Stewart Hardman, South
Yorkshire 1985 / 1989.
Go Go – Jackie Topham and Bernadine Wood
Dagenham, Essex 1985.
Northern Mod Scene – Martin Dixon,
Scarborough 1979.

northern
mod

scene   30P

HAVE A GOOD TIME

MODZINE

ISSUE 7   50p

HAVE A GOOD TIME

ISSUE 1.

Interviews
with.

THE
GENTS.

The.
MOMENT.
+
CHARTS.

REVIEWS.

And
MORE.

"To be honest, I have so many mod memories and so many of them came about because I had made the decision to edit my own fanzine. In my head I am still attending [all those events] now. The Rotherham Mod All-dayer, Clifton Hall, 1985 – The Gents and Yeh-Yeh played. I had been to other mod-related events but this was the first real, full-blown one. Seeing so many mod girls in attendance – and the fashion! Riding overnight on my first scooter to the Isle of Wight to see The Action play. Cruising down the Rhine at the Linz rally. Seeing my mate's band Los Flechazos [from León, Spain] play in England for the very first time. A minibus with The Most to play in the south of France, which was a real crazy weekend! The Scarborough Mod Rally, 1986, the Lemon Tree, so many mods involved in the birth of Britpop – wow, a new band called The Clique playing! Blackpool Winter Gardens Baronial Hall – a mega-venue, as was Gorleston Ocean Rooms. An all-dayer at the Hippodrome in Central London – those bar prices, how much??? (Well, this was 1987!). DJ'ing for the first time ever on a rally in Spain, after that first record – I loved the experience. Rally evenings when walking to the venue and heads turned looking at what everyone was wearing. That feeling when riding into a seaside town and the scooter cruise along the seafront. Meeting so many really good friends over the years. My fanzine sent me off on this journey and I regret nothing!"

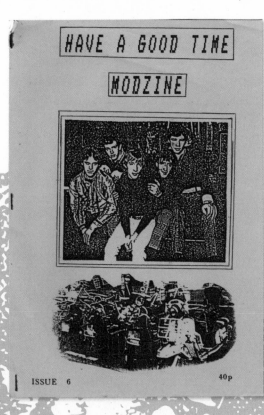

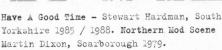

Have A Good Time – Stewart Hardman, South Yorkshire 1985 / 1988. Northern Mod Scene Martin Dixon, Scarborough 1979.

'ALL AROUND THE WORLD':

THE MOD
INTERNATIONALISTS

Real Emotion – Sean O'Gorman
and Peter Delvin, Dublin
Ireland 1983.

Real Emotion.

ISSUE NO.1.

*THE TIMES*ANTHONY MEYNELL INTERVIEW*TRAMORE PIX*THE BLADES*

Ireland was closely connected to the British mod scene and, rather surprisingly, given that the Troubles were at their peak in the early eighties, there was a strong connection between the mods in the north and their southern counterparts. Fans travelled on the armoured train between the two capitals, Dublin and Belfast, or even on scooters to gigs and dances either side of the border (a journey I personally undertook on my Vespa in 1983, armed with a bag of records and a sheaf of *Extraordinary Sensations* to sell).

The island was also a fertile ground for editors; the Irish scene might have been a year or two behind its UK cousin, but what its adherents lacked in timing, they made up for in sheer enthusiasm.

Sean O'Gorman was heavily involved in the Dublin mod scene and was a founder member of the Emerald Society, a collective for Irish mods that was loosely modelled on Mark Johnson's Phoenix Society (see page 150). Sean was manager of the band Instant Party and, together with band member Peter Devlin, he established and edited *Real Emotion* in the early eighties. Named after a song by Ireland's leading mod band The Blades, the fanzine featured contributions from fellow Instant Party member, Ken Sweeney, who is now an award-winning journalist.

Sean remembers: "Ireland had a vibrant scene in the early eighties that mirrored the UK but on a smaller scale. The mod scene in Dublin was originally centred around two weekly mod nights in Bubbles, but soon there were clubs popping up with recurring frequency. There was also an exciting live music circuit based around The Blades and Instant Party, with groups like The Scene, Makin' Time and The Rage visiting from the UK. This led to a lot of interaction between mods from all over Ireland, with groups coming down from Belfast for gigs and the mods from Ireland making similar reverse trips. During a time of sectarian issues north of the border, it was great to see that mod overcame and ignored all the issues that came with the Troubles; instead, it was all about clothes, music and having a good time."

Like so many fanzines at the time, *Real Emotion* ran for only three issues, the final one being prepared but not making it into print.

Robbie MacDonald founded Dublin's *Change The World* in the mid-eighties. "When I first set up the fanzine, the mod world in Dublin was going through a bit of a hard time. Bubbles, the original Dublin mod club – which I first went to when I was just 13 – had gone through some traumatic changes following the emerging fashion for scooter boys. The DJs had started playing psychobilly and I felt that I had to make some kind of statement to galvanise the mod scene back to the kind of things we were into. I wanted to let people know what was still going on, as it was getting a bit lost with all the King Kurt and The Meteors rock stuff. Me and my mates just couldn't get into that sound.

ISSUE No.2

ISSUE 3.

Real Emotion — Sean O'Gorman
and Peter Delvin, Dublin
Ireland 1983/1984. Dublin Mods.

Change The World - Robbie and Steven
McDonald, Dublin 1983.
Start - Manfred Breiner, Austria 1983.

"Like many people in Ireland, I had been inspired by **Extraordinary Sensations** and I wanted to spread the good news and actually prove to myself that I could [make a fanzine myself]. There had only been a few fanzines in Ireland up to that point (I suppose **Reflections** had been the main one). I ended up selling approximately 300 copies of both issues, quite a few when I popped up to Belfast for gigs and club nights. There was a bit of cross-pollination between north and south at the time, and we wanted the scene to come together even more. It was strange because you had quite a few people who wouldn't come to Emerald Society parties at the time, even though we always went to theirs. I suppose I was hoping that a fanzine could unite people somewhat. I felt that fanzines are like a virus that spreads ideas.

"Homer* was a good mate of mine and he started doing **Esoteric** soon after. We eventually held our first Change The World all-dayer and it was really successful, just what I was hoping would happen. We were only admitting mods and keeping out people who didn't share our values as, quite simply, we were mods and they weren't. The fanzine name was taken from a Small World song, and indeed the band were featured on the cover too."

"I eventually stopped the fanzine because I was actually becoming much more competent at graphic design and had decided I wanted to do it as a career. I had produced around half of Issue 3 but then made the big decision to move to London and look for work. The fanzine just ran out of steam!"

While things were going well in Ireland, by 1983 the rest of Europe was awash with burgeoning underground mod scenes.

Henry Storch, owner of the Unique Club and record label in Düsseldorf, remembers how important UK fanzines were in spreading the word about the scene outside of Britain.

"I can't stress enough how important the UK fanzines were to the German mod scene. In the mid-eighties we were into the garage rock sound of The Sonics and The Prisoners and fanzines were a lifeline to what was going on with new bands and events. You could pick up the occasional copy in one of the independent record shops but more often than not you had to write off to them, which could be difficult, as it meant you had to get hold of some English pounds. So it wasn't too long before we were producing our own German modzines. There were some good ones based in Vienna, too. They had a healthy scene in Austria, the main fanzines being **Snoter II** and **Start**, the latter of which was edited by Manfred Breiner, Austria's main face, who was better known as The Elk."

This lifeline to the UK was equally important once the northern soul influence had taken hold of the scene, as Henry explains further.

START

START NR 8   WINTER   83   S:30

*Homer, better known as the movie soundtrack producer David Holmes, was one of the main DJs and events organisers in Belfast at the time. He also produced **Psychotic Reaction** in 1982 with his friend David McNamee, but it only lasted for one issue before changing fashions in the mod world led them to start again with **Esoteric** a year later.

"We soon embraced the northern soul scene here in Germany and the first ever all-nighter was run in Hamburg by Olaf Ott and Leif Nueske from Fab Records. The trouble was, we didn't really have a clue about the music over here, as it was a totally new thing. Many of the British fanzines printed lists and charts, which were very useful in getting a feel for this new sound. Buying the records in Germany wasn't difficult, as there were lots of soul record shops and there was a strong American presence because of the US Army being stationed here, but you had to know what to buy. Ian Clark from Kent Records used to write a column in *Extraordinary Sensations* full of the latest discoveries and when they published Randy Cozens' Mod Top 100*, it really did provide us with an important DJ guide."

Antonio Bacciocchi, better known on the Italian scene as Tony Face, continues: "I set up my modzine *Faces* with my mate Alfred Cancellieri in 1980 and it ran for 17 issues over four years. We were based in a small town called Piacenza, which is not far from Milan, but we used to cover all the news from the mod scene in Italy and abroad with reviews and stories about the scene and the mod style. I used to keep an eye on what was going on in the UK so Italian mods could follow the latest bands and record releases. The fanzine was a lot of work, so from 1984 we stopped it and established a monthly mod newsletter called *Sweetest Feeling* instead."

Like so many fanzine editors, Tony became the centre of his own mod community. "I was one of the first mods in Italy, as early as 1978, and *Faces* was the first national modzine, distributed all over the country, selling around 500 copies per issue. We were involved with the first Italian mod runs** in Viareggio and Rimini from 1983, and in the mid-eighties, I brought British bands like The Moment, The Rage, Direct Hits and The Times over to tour. Very successful tours they were too, as we had a vibrant scene with many of our own Italian bands gaining national success."

Also from Italy was *Modern Outlook*. Set up by Bruno Pisa, who was based in Pordenone, it ran from 1983 for a total of 13 issues.

"The first three editions were more of a newsletter than a proper fanzine, just both sides of an A4 sheet. Soon I enlarged it into a proper fanzine. We had a very exciting mod scene in Italy in the mid-eighties and *Modern Outlook* was just one of a whole collection that kept the people informed about what was going on. I also featured many bands from the sixties, as it was important to inform and educate!"

This pattern was repeated across Europe. Greece had a particularly strong mod community and mods were even appearing behind the Iron Curtain. I myself DJ'd in East Berlin in 1984 and there was a smattering of mods in the small bar, although I am not aware that there were any fanzines being produced there. Russia, too, harboured a very small but enthusiastic mod scene in Moscow and Leningrad.

ORGANO D'INFORMAZIONE DEL MOVIMENTO MOD ITALIANO N°7

FACES

*Randy Cozens was an original sixties mod with a passion for soul music, who wrote letter after letter to the established music press, pleading for mods to 'check the soul heritage of their mod forefathers'. *Sounds* eventually allowed him to compile a chart of his favourite mod soul records, which became the Mod Top 100. Randy also established the legendary 6Ts Soul Club with his friend Ady Croasdell.

**Mod runs and scooter rallies are still a typically British sight, usually on Bank Holidays, as hundreds, sometimes thousands, of mods gather to ride en masse to a particular town or festival.

Faces – Antonio 'Tony Face' Bacciocchi
and Alfred Cancellieri, Italy 1980/1984.
Modern Outlook – Bruno Pisa, Italy 1983/1996.

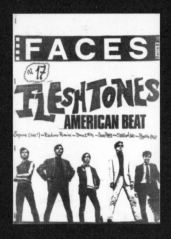

Faces – Antonio 'Tony Face' Bacciocchi and
Alfred Cancellieri, Italy 1980/1984.
Modern Outlook – Bruno Pisa, Italy 1983/1996.

ORGANO INFORMATIVO MODERNISTA
N°8 £1000

FACES

Letraset
SPAREMATIC
heat resistant

pennarex

MOD É VITA

GET OUT

GLORY DAYS   CHARTS

ACID JAZZ

REVIEWS

N.1 DICEMBRE 88 COPIA GRATUITA

So Smart !

Smarten up

THE JAM   BRIDGE HOUSE RECORDS

Record & Tape
Exchange

QUADRO PHENIA

38 Notting Hill Gate
London, W.11

...bridge Road
Notting Hill Gate
London, W.11

90 Goldhawk Road
Shepherd's Bush
London, W.12

BEAT

So Smart !

quint afoo...

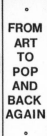

Die
DIRECT HITS
Story

4 DM

FROM
ART
TO
POP
AND
BACK
AGAIN

•

TEIL
1

•

Geschichten
aus dem
britischen
Beat-,
Pop-
und
Psychedelia-
Untergrund
der
80er Jahre

•

von Armin Müller

THE JETSET

4 DM

FROM
ART
TO
POP
AND
BACK
AGAIN

•

TEIL
2

•

Geschichten
aus dem
britischen
Beat-,
Pop-
und
Psychedelia-
Untergrund
der
80er Jahre

•

(Fast)
alles über
ihre Platten,
ihr Label,
ihre Kleider,
ihre Comics
und
ihr Auto

von Armin Müller

Get Out – Antonio
'Tony Face' Bacciocchi,
Italy 1988.
So Smart – Antonio
'Tony Face' Bacciocchi,
Italy 1985.
Smarten Up – Germany
Die Direct Hits – Armin
Müller, Germany 1988.
The Jetset – Armin
Müller, Germany 1988.

Scandinavia was not immune either. Maria Lindén was founder and editor of **Gloria Ladies International**, the mouthpiece of the Gloria Ladies Association, which was an all-female collective of mods, original-style skinheads and swinging sixties girls in Sweden.

"From 1990 to 1992 we were the first ever 'all-girl' club organisers on the Swedish scene and we had members from all around the world. The fanzine was an extension of the society, something for the members to read, and was edited by me along with Josephine Rogo and Lena Högberg. It also allowed me to promote my DJ'ing, which I did with my friend Asa; we were the first-ever female DJs in Sweden, where we went by the name of The Glory Girls! Sweden had a healthy scene so we sold the fanzine at gigs and on Swedish scooter rallies. Many of the copies went out via the post."

One of the most prolific European fanzines was *Reacciones*. Edited by Ringo Julian, it ran for a total of 18 issues, from the spring of 1984 to November 1988. Ringo was one of the first mods in Barcelona, Spain, the city that was home to another important mover and shaker on the scene, DJ Eneida Fever. The most important mod organiser in Spain, she set up tons of events throughout the revival years. What becomes apparent is that strong scenes produced strong fanzines, which in turn boosted local markets, providing encouragement – and endless source material – for editors to continue producing new issues.

Beyond Europe, this same cycle was occurring across the world, and nowhere more so than in Australia. There were healthy mod scenes in both Sydney and Melbourne and to a lesser extent in the other states. At the time, there was a thriving live music scene in the country and an extremely healthy live circuit in the larger cities.*

Bands like The Sets, Stupidity and the Allniters commanded enormous live followings. This threw up dozens of interesting and important zines, most notably *Get Smart*, which was edited by Anita Janelsins, and *Shake And Shout*, which was edited by Steve Dettre (now one of Australia's foremost sports journalists) and Glyn Williams, and ran from 1979 to around 1983.

The Sydney mod scene was the most organised I had personally come across, and centred on regular nights at the Quarryman's Hotel. This level of professionalism was reflected in *Shake And Shout*, which was fully typeset from the very beginning, making it way ahead of the UK competition. Its editors also pioneered the Australian and New Zealand mod 'targets',** which I saw everywhere during my first visit to the country at the behest of Steve and Glyn.

Glyn Williams had originally edited his own mod fanzine, *GoGoGoing*, along with Donna McKenna from the mod band Donna & The Daydreams.

*This was based mainly on the fact that, unlike the UK, Australia didn't have a nightclub culture; instead, the large Victorian pubs in Australia's major cities would have bands regularly playing in the corner.

**The Aussie version of the traditional mod target featured a kangaroo in the centre, while the New Zealand version featured a kiwi.

Reacciones — Ringo Julian, Spain 1984/1985.
Gloria Ladies Association — Maria Lindén, Sweden 1990.

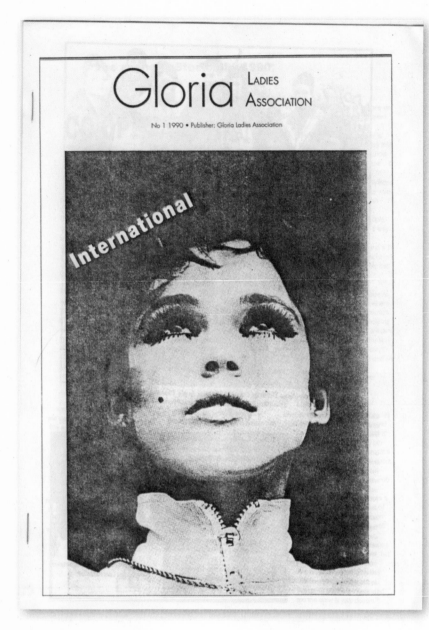

Gloria LADIES ASSOCIATION

No 1 1990 • Publisher: Gloria Ladies Association

International

Gloria

INTERNATIONAL   No 3 1991

N 51

DIZY

Six *Exciting* reasons   N°1
why you must see Britain!   20 frs

The Jam   9 Below Zero

Purple Hearts   Dolly Mixture   Long Tall Shorty

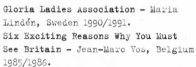

Gloria Ladies Association – Maria
Lindén, Sweden 1990/1991.
Six Exciting Reasons Why You Must
See Britain – Jean-Marc Vos, Belgium
1985/1986.

Gloria
INTERNATIONAL   No 4 1992

FASHION SPECIAL

MADE IN SWEDEN

Reacciones - Ringo Julian, Spain
1984/1985.
Reasons Why You Must See Britain
Jean-Marc Vos, Belgium 1985/1986.
Pow! - Philippe de Vienne
France, 1984.
Start - France.

"We only published one issue at the beginning of 1980 and when I joined forces with Steve Dettre it was no more, and Anita's superb *Get Smart* took over from where we left off."

Photographer David Tytherleigh remembers his own forays into the world of the Oz mod fanzine: "I tried to do something different from a normal modzine. I wouldn't have really classed myself as a proper mod; I was rather someone who was interested in the overall scene – the music, the clothes and scooters. I was on holiday in the UK back in 1984 and went on a scooter run to Great Yarmouth. I had an amazing time, and as soon as I returned I bought myself a Vespa PX. I was just getting into photography and wanted to give something back to the scene so I put together several fanzines of my mod photos and sold them outside venues. I used a different title for each issue, like *Sydney Mods*, *Mod OK* and *Uptight*."

The high standards continued well into the late nineties and early 21st-century with the professionally typeset *Modern Times*, 'the magazine for mods', edited by Kelvin Madden in Toowong, Queensland, but distributed nationally. Issue 5 contained a detailed appraisal of the life and career of the unrivalled Australian face Don Hosie, who, along with his brother, Gary, and through their bands The Sets, Stupidity and The Mustard Club, remained the backbone of the scene until Don's untimely and tragic death in a car accident at the turn of the millennium.

While small pockets of mod have always existed in South and Central America, in countries as diverse as Peru, Argentina, Venezuela and Mexico, the main outbreak of American modernism during the eighties occurred on the US West Coast.

Bart Mendoza, Manual Scan frontman and one of the foremost movers and shakers on the US mod scene, explains how it happened.

"It's hard to pinpoint when the mod scene kicked off on the West Coast. There were already a few mods in southern California by the late 1970s, as well as bands like The Crawdaddys, which were popular with mods like Greg Shaw.* What really blew things up was the release of *Quadrophenia* and I also think that the early eighties media's fascination with the sixties look and scooters definitely helped spread the word – there were numerous afternoon TV and radio news reports and newspaper articles about mod events and scooter rallies. This all filtered out to surrounding and like-minded communities.

"Personally, as a teenager I liked the sixties look due to a love of The Who, The Zombies and The Lovin' Spoonful. I did some intern work in 1978 at local radio station KPRI. They gave me all the promo singles they received but weren't going to play. Thus, I discovered The Jam, and things grew from there. Their concerts were catalysts for a lot of activity, as were visits from Secret Affair and, later, Anthony Meynell and his band Squire, who

Shake And Shout – Steve Dettre, (and later) Glyn Williams, Sydney, Australia 1980/1983.
Go Go Going – Glyn Williams and Donna McKenna Sydney, Australia, 1980.
Get Smart – Anita Janelsins, Sydney, Ausdtralia 1984. Modern Times – Kelvin Madden, Queensland, Australia 1998.

*Greg Shaw was an influential tastemaker on the US West Coast. His fanzine, *Who Put The Bomp* (or simply *Bomp!*) championed the emerging garage rock revival as well as the Paisley Underground scene of the eighties. During the mid-seventies, his label Bomp! Records released material by Iggy Pop, The Crawdaddys and Devo, among others.

Photo Fanzine
Mid 1980's

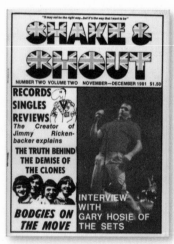

Shake And Shout - Steve Dettre, Sydney, Australia 1980/1982.
Modern Times - Kelvin Madden, Queensland,
Australia 1999/2000.

Sydney Mods, Uptight, Mod OK - David Tytherleigh
Sydney, Australia 1985/1986.
Shake And Shout - Steve Dettre (and later) Glyn Williams,
Sydney, Australia 1981/1982.

Ready! Steady! Read! – San Francisco, USA.
Twist – Dave Lumian and Philip Cramer
Los Angeles, USA 1983. Making Tyme – Mick Hale,
New Jersey, USA 1985.
Wha-a-am! – Elizabeth Pepin, San Francisco,
USA 1983/1989. Hippy Hippy Shake – Carrie Swing,
Berkeley, USA 1987/1989.
Sound Affects Underground – Bart Mendoza,
San Diego, USA 1988.

played over here a number of times. UK fanzines also made it over here occasionally; I used to distribute **In The Crowd** direct from the UK, but whenever Squire played in San Diego, Tony Meynell would bring a suitcase of British fanzines with him to sell. That kept us up to date with what was going on in the UK."

It wasn't just San Diego that had its own burgeoning mod scene; things were also heating up in Orange County, Los Angeles, San Francisco, Chicago, Minneapolis and New Jersey, with smaller groups in most other major cities. There was strong camaraderie between the local scenes, with bands trading gigs and fanzine editors offering places for their contemporaries to crash during events. Scooter clubs, including the Secret Society from San Diego and San Francisco, 100 Faces from Los Angeles and the Dancing Skeletons from Chula Vista, also lent their support to mod events up and down the West Coast.

Like with a lot of regional scenes, most US mod fanzines ran for just one or two issues. The major standouts were **Wha-a-am** from San Francisco, which was edited by Elizabeth Pepin* and her crew, and **Twist Magazine**, which was based in Los Angeles and created by Dave Lumian, who, at that time, was manager of the biggest American mod band, The Untouchables. These were pretty much professional fanzines with proper distribution deals and they were available at places like Tower Records.

There were also the Xeroxed and stapled fanzines, including my own **Sound Affects**, which ran to nine issues, and **Ready Steady Read**, which was also from the Bay Area. The guitarist from the band Mod Fun, Mick Hale, edited **Making Tyme**, while other local fanzines included **Directions**, **Voxed In**, **Purple Flashes** and **Contact**.

The local live music scene was also thriving, although only a handful of these bands toured. The mod scene also peaked at the same time as the new psychedelic movement, which the US media referred to as 'the paisley underground'. Most mods, however, saw no real distinction – bands like The Bangs (who later morphed into international chart-toppers The Bangles), The Three O'Clock and The Plimsouls were regarded as just as mod as The Untouchables, Mod Fun, Manual Scan, The Event, Modest Proposal, The Question, The Dig and Chardon Square. The USA also had an active garage scene that included bands like The Nashville Ramblers, The Tell-Tale Hearts, The J-Walkers and The Funseekers.

However, by the end of the decade, the scene in the USA had gone into decline. It's hard to say exactly why – it was probably a combination of factors. Although The Event's 'Pop-Think-In' [from the album *This Is The Event*] and Manual Scan's *Lost Sessions* were both released in 1989, and the New Sounds Festival that year drew well over a thousand fans, gentrification in cities led to a steep rise in rents and many music venues had to close. Lots of the original crowd had moved on to careers or families,

*Elizabeth Pepin published and edited **Wha-a-am** from 1982 to 1986 and also promoted many Bay Area live shows. Today, she is a documentary filmmaker, researcher and writer, and is perhaps best known for her hugely popular surf photography.

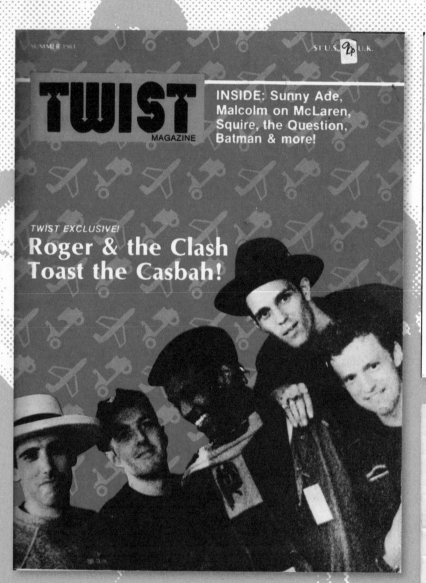

the original bands split and public interest in the music, always fickle at best, generally declined, especially in those early post-MTV years.

Things never died out completely, though. A few scooter clubs rode on, including the Secret Society. Within a few years, bands formed like New Jersey mod power trio The Insomniacs and mod-rock group The Shambles, which later featured Bart Mendoza as guitarist/singer. Mike Stax* was hosting his Hipsters events in San Diego, while there were plenty of mod DJ nights in Los Angeles and elsewhere. And let's not forget the cultural phenomenon that is Austin Powers: International Man of Mystery…!, the 1997 film parody that satirised London's sixties mod scene and brought mod – albeit an extremely kitsch version – to a whole new generation.

As the eighties wore on, the mod scene exploded in a way that the 1979 originators could never have envisaged.

*Mike moved from the UK to San Diego, California, in 1981 to join The Crawdaddys. In 1983, he launched the magazine *Ugly Things*, which covered sixties beat, garage and psych music.

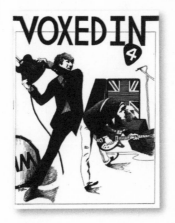

Twist – Dave Lumian and Philip Cramer,
Los Angeles, USA 1983.
Scooters & Reggae – Kevin Fingier,
Argentina 2010.
Voxed In – Scott Harper (RIP), San Diego,
USA 1986/1991.
Making Tyme – Mick Hale, New Jersey,
USA 1986.

Sawdust Caesars – Chris Canigiula, San Luis Obispo, USA 1987/1988.
Wha-a-am! – Elizabeth Pepin, San Francisco, USA 1983/1989.
Hippy Hippy Shake – Carrie Swing, Berkeley, USA 1987/1989.
The Reaction – Jason Morris, Toronto, Canada 1983.

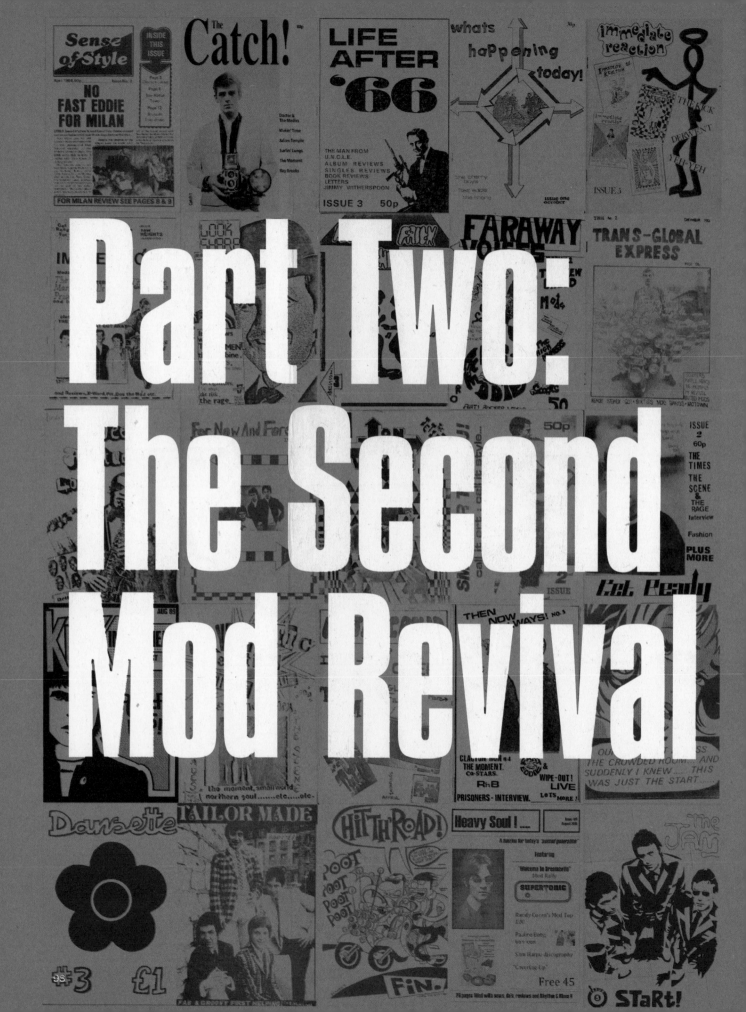

Part Two: The Second Mod Revival

'PERFECT WORLD':

THE SECOND WAVE

In December 1982, Paul Weller had called time on The Jam. Looking at the scene in broad terms, that single act should really have been the end of it. Most of the original revival bands had already thrown in the towel, frustrated by the lack of coverage and genuine vilification they faced from the established music press. It was easier to name the bands who hadn't split than the ones who had.

Of the main originators, Squire were the only ones still making records. Long Tall Shorty and the R&B-influenced Fast Eddie were holding up their end on the live scene and Small World, latecomers that they were, found themselves moved to the fore. There were exceptions to the rule, however. Dennis Greaves, lead singer and guitarist of the mod-leaning rhythm and blues band Nine Below Zero, realised that The Jam's split might provide an opportunity, so in the early months of 1983 he established a new mod band, The Truth. Soon signed to the quasi-major IRS Records, the band managed to galvanise what was left of the original revival mods and introduce a new generation of mod kids to live music. Chart hits like 'A Step In The Right Direction' and 'Confusion (Hits Us Every Time)' soon followed.

A new mod scene was starting to take shape; the Electric Stadium and the Regency Suite were the Essex-based clubs, the Ilford Palais mod all-dayers were a galvanising force, too, and Tony Class (more on him later) was thriving with his South and West London mod discos.

Then, in 1983, Paul Weller surprised everyone again. He had caused much wailing and tribulation by breaking up The Jam at their absolute peak, but within six months he'd established a new group. The Style Council was a collective that featured Paul's then wife, singer Dee C. Lee, the teenage jazz drummer Steve White and a man with impeccable mod credentials, keyboard player Mick Talbot. Originally pianist with The Merton Parkas, Mick had also performed with The Jam and The Chords, as well as the incredibly soulful Dexy's Midnight Runners.

Paul Weller stated from the beginning that his new band's sound was the very future of mod. The Style Council would embrace both soul and jazz in a way that hadn't been possible through the musical restrictions imposed on a three-piece with a background in speed-fuelled R&B and punk anthems. At first, hundreds of thousands of Jam fans around the world appeared to be in some kind of collective shock and, initially at least, very few realised what Weller was attempting to do with this new direction (which, incidentally, mirrored the move towards northern soul that was currently gripping the mod world). But soon fans were convinced, and The Style Council infused a new determination in the next generation of mods. Perhaps they had adopted the revival as very young teens off the back of 2 tone in 1980 and '81, but The Style Council gave them something more contemporary to follow.

Actor Martin Freeman, then in his early teens, remembers the impact Weller's new band had on him.

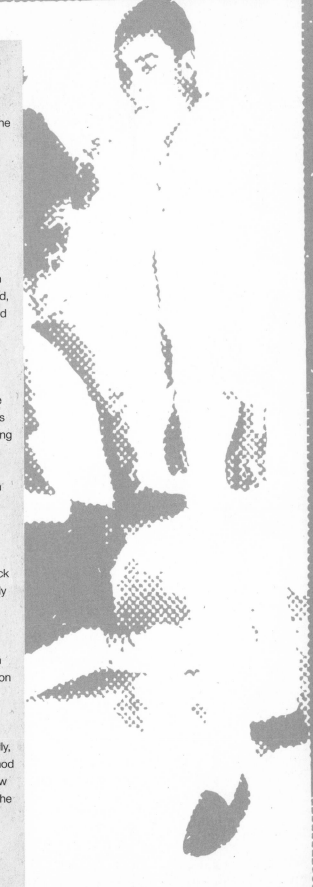

"The Style Council were a revelation. They were outward-looking, open and occasionally funny. Brave, both musically and politically, and even well bloody dressed. They were natural for me. Inspirational even."

Record label boss Dean Rudland, himself a 13-year-old Jam and sixties music fan, recalls his feeling about Weller's new direction.

"In the last year of The Jam and the first year of The Style Council Paul Weller was talking up a large variety of mod influences, which the original revival mods of '79 and '80 had ignored. By '83 many of those originals had drifted away and you were left with a hardcore rump of 22-year-olds who were prepared to dig deeper and go with it. Jazz, poetry, film – I mean just look at the cover of *Our Favourite Shop**. This was a man determined to push his agenda and open up the mod scene to new ideas and influences. This dovetailed with our personal rejection of all new music (bad) in favour of sixties soul and R&B (good), as played by the likes of DJs Paul Hallam and Toski at clubs like Sneakers. Of course, both specific ideas merged a year or so later, by which time the new mod revival was definitely underway and throwing up the next generation of bands, like The Untouchables, The Prisoners, Makin' Time and Fast Eddie."

Hallam remembers the shift from the original revival mods to the new generation: "I started going to mod clubs like Cheeky Pete's in Richmond or the Bush Hotel in Shepherd's Bush in 1980, aged around 15. Everything seemed to be very band-driven back then, with the DJs playing a large amount of sixties pop, things like Shocking Blue's version of 'Venus' or 'Can't Explain' by The Who. To be honest, we were bored of that and a few of us got into the type of music championed by Guy Stevens and his super rare sixties label Sue. At this point we weren't aware of the East London mods, who had their own, similar clubs at the Regency in Ilford and Scamps in Southend. We just wanted to dig deeper, rarer and darker – less miniskirts and more original sixties mod ethos.

"For many of the original '79 crowd, I think they treated the mod revival as just a passing phase, like rockabilly or casual that both came along soon after it… Many of my older peers who had stuck with the scene – people like Eddie Piller, Tony 'Mappy' Hayzer, Bob Morris or Ray Margetson – had been involved with the mod revival for at least five years by then and were looking for something different too. This all seemed to come together in the spring of '84, when the vision of the remaining revival mods joined with that of the new generation. It might not have been a bigger revival, but the mid-eighties scene was certainly more committed and intense, and it was national in a way that '79 hadn't been."

Hallam's mid-eighties surge came about because the new generation of bands, like Fast Eddie and Makin' Time, dovetailed perfectly with the next wave of DJs, who were much more influenced by soul and original rhythm and blues. In other words, music that was aimed at the dance floor.

* *Our Favourite Shop* was The Style Council's second studio album, released on June 8, 1985. The album cover consisted of a black and white photo of the band standing in a 'shop', which featured merchandise that represented their influences, including Blue Note LP sleeves, seventies soul albums, an Otis Redding T-shirt, a book of Tony Hancock scripts and a selection of Chelsea football programmes.

Sense of Style

April 1984, 60p _____ **Issue No. 2**

NO FAST EDDIE FOR MILAN

ESSEX based rhythm & soul band Fast Eddie missed out on an Italian mini tour three days before the visit.

Fast Eddie plus 40 odd London mods were destined for the International Mod Festival reported in last months Sense of Style. The band were due to play 3 nights with Tony Class D-Jaying as well.

The Saturday was to see Fast Eddie topping the bill in a gig involving several other Italian bands. On the Monday prior to the trip, Tony Class, the organiser, was informed that the fares of the band could not be paid by the Italian promotors. This came about when sponsors pulled out of the event.

Despite the absense of the English band the event went off (in the truest sense) with four Italian bands on the bill for Saturday night. A further trip to either Italy or Spain is scheduled for September.

FOR MILAN REVIEW SEE PAGES 8 & 9

FOR MILAN REVIEW SEE PAGES 8 & 9

Sense of Style — Paul Hallam and Mick Mouskos, Middlesex 1984.

Hallam again: "I think that in society in general things were quite tough in the UK around this time, so the kids who came to Sneakers or the Outrigger in Birmingham wanted a type of escapism. The whole country wanted escapism and the new generation of 19-year-old mods was no different – they dressed up, they spent all their money on clothes and records, and to an extent they made a conscious effort to reject contemporary society, dreaming and dressing up – like Hank Jacobs once said, 'You were so far away.'

"We stopped [my fanzine] after just two issues because by March 1984 I was riding the crest of a DJ wave, playing out five nights' a week. I just didn't have the time…"

Sth Circular — Chris Hayward and Andy Ford,
London 1980/1981.
Angry Voices — Alan, Eastleigh 1985.
Beat That! — Jez Slowe, High Wycombe 1981/1982.

Angry Voices – Alan, Eastleigh 1985.
007 – Paul Field, London 1985.
Empty Dreams – Neil, Kent.
Time Moves Us On – Robin King, Chichester 1985.
Cool And Collected – Tim Boden 1984.

'TIME FOR ACTION':

PRODUCTION AND DISTRIBUTION

Maximum Speed – Goffa Gladding, Clive Reams
and Kim Gault, London 1979.

The reason why fanzines were so attractive to youngsters and why so many tried their hand at editing one was because they were so simple to make, produce and distribute. All that was needed was access to a typewriter, printer and photocopier, and bags of enthusiasm.

The fanzine editor's basic tool was a typewriter. Very few fanzines were handwritten due to both practical and stylistic reasons; handwritten pages (as many teachers will tell you) are hard to read, while the individual and often idiosyncratic styles of multiple contributors could appear scruffy and non-uniform. There was little point in writing articles if they couldn't be easily read or they looked rubbish.

"We never got as serious as typesetting at *Maximum Speed* but I did try and make it look as professional as I could with a typewriter. There were often handwritten annotations and lots of cut-and-paste ideas," remembers Goffa Gladding.

I remember: "Typewriters still provided the main form of block copy in those pre-word processor days. We started *Extraordinary Sensations* on a bashed-about old Remington typewriter, but by the time Terry Rawlings joined the editorial staff, we had turned to a pair of clunky old 3M electric models."

Rawlings continues the story: "I remember thinking how cool and advanced we were because the electric typewriters had an interchangeable golf ball arrangement instead of the old 'letters on sticks' scenario. You could change the golf ball and use an alternative one with a different typeface size or even italics. We thought this was incredibly advanced. Of course, the Amstrad computer hadn't been invented by then!"

Next on the list for any would-be fanzine editor's toolbox were a pair of scissors, a Pritt Stick and a bottle of Copydex – in other words, the early 'cut-and-paste' toolkit. Teenage fanzine editors understood nothing of copyright law – which protects an artist's intellectual property rights over

ISSUE NUMBER NINE~THIRTY PENCE

"THE BITTEREST PILL I'VE EVER HAD TO SWALLOW"

EXTRAORDINARY SENSATIONS
CHRISTMAS 1982

Extraordinary Sensations Eddie Piller
and Terry Rawlings, Essex 1982.

his creation, whether it be literary, dramatic, musical or artistic – and if they did, they cared even less. So, armed with their weapons of choice, virtually every single mod revival fanzine filled up its pages with other people's photos and drawings (sixties cartoons of Batman were extremely popular).

I recall: "For the *Extraordinary Sensations* issue that covered The Jam's split, which was released in January 1983 and subtitled 'The Bitterest Pill I Ever Had To Swallow', we quite literally took a birthday card that featured a pencil drawing (albeit a superb drawing) of Paul Weller, cut it out and stuck it to the front cover with some Letraset* words surrounding it. Of course, it would have contravened copyright law but to be honest we didn't know any better. Whether the actual artist who drew the card ever noticed, I never found out, but the number of copies featuring Weller's face that made it onto the streets would have certainly outstripped the original card's sales by thousands (10,000, to be exact).

"Much later, the original image made it into the Jam exhibition in London's Somerset House, where it was positioned right next to that issue of *Extraordinary Sensations* for which we had purloined it. To be honest, if I had known about the law or even the fairness of using the picture, we wouldn't have done it. But I didn't. It didn't even occur to me."

Rawlings again: "I always reckoned that [Roy] Lichtenstein's take on pop art was a major influence on many mod fanzines, even if it was subconscious. Purple Hearts purloined a Lichtensteinesque image for the front cover of their *Frustration* 45 single and Tony Lordan blatantly robbed the Lambretta typeface for their logo. People were always cut-and-pasting cartoon images but then changing the words in the speech bubbles. I suppose it was an easy way to get a message across. Drawing your own cartoons from scratch was very time-consuming, although as time went on, it was something we did more and more in *Extraordinary Sensations*. To people whose full-time job wasn't editing a fanzine, I reckon they wouldn't have been able to devote the resources – so nicking a cartoon from a 20-year-old copy of *Superman* was an easy choice."

The artistic integrity of mod fanzines stayed broadly consistent until the mid-eighties. Up to this point the concept of typesetting was an arcane science, known only to professional printers or graphic designers. It was a regular factor in editors abandoning their magazines because, quite simply, print in the 1980s was difficult to source and almost prohibitively expensive. The advent of computer technology soon changed that and opened up the world of professional layouts, not necessarily to the uninitiated but certainly to mods with a background in the art.

Chris Hunt on the production of *Shadows And Reflections*: "The first issue was just photocopied with a print run of 125, but by Issue 2 I'd found a print company that could handle the numbers I wanted at a decent

*Letraset made sheets of transferable typography and graphics. Architects, designers, artists and, of course, fanzine editors relied on Letraset's huge range of typefaces, from classic to contemporary, to bring a professional look to their work before the advent of desktop publishing.

THE MEDICS

price. Issue 3 came with a Dance Network flexi-disc – and by Issue 4 it had become the first glossy mod fanzine. It peaked at 2,000 sales before I finally pulled the plug on it. In terms of its presentation, I kind of wanted it to look like a proper magazine with type in columns, which took a little bit of ingenuity back in those days. My final fanzine, **The Catch!**, which followed Issue 6 of **Shadows And Reflections**, was my first fanzine that used proper typesetting."

Paul Hallam, the West London DJ behind the hugely popular Sneakers night, held weekly at the Shepherd's Bush Hotel, used his practical typesetting experience to produce one of the first-ever examples of a mod 'magazine', rather than a fanzine. Called **A Sense Of Style**, it surfaced at the end of 1983 in a compact A5 format with a professional look.

In a similar vein, and even slightly earlier, was Wayne Iredale's **Life After '66**, from Leicester. Iredale used his day job in graphic design as a means of creating a more professional end result. But these two were the exception rather than the rule, and right up until the general decline of the mod fanzine in the early nineties, the cut-and-paste method was the one editors favoured, mainly for its simplicity and affordability.

Hallam, who started **Sense Of Style** with Mick Mouskos in 1983, was pushed to start his own fanzine as a direct result of mainstream indifference.

"I remember very specifically why me and Mick started the fanzine. Firstly, we had taken over the Bush Hotel for our Sneakers night, we had sent a press release to every single contemporary music and listings paper, including **Time Out**, but received nothing. Not a single mention, anywhere… it incensed me. We realised that we would get more attention for our events if we targeted mods rather than trying to interest the mainstream press. By '83 our world was completely underground: we had slipped under the mainstream radar."

But Hallam, as a full-time typesetter, wanted his fanzine to stand out from the crowd.

"I wanted to make a magazine, a proper magazine, like **The Face**. I didn't want to write about Jackie Wilson or The Action, I didn't want to review the new Squire album… I didn't want it to look like it was a fifth-form art O-level project. I reckoned that our punters would rather read about what was going on in our world – who was DJ'ing here, who had fallen out with who, but, most importantly, we wanted it to look like a real magazine, and my experience as a printer and typesetter meant that we could make that happen.

"The first headline story for **A Sense Of Style** was actually news, not just some collage of sixties pictures. We interviewed Eddie Piller about him

The Catch! 80p

Doctor & The Medics

Makin' Time

Julian Temple

Surfin' Lungs

The Moment

Ray Brooks

Catch 1

Shadows And Reflections – Chris Hunt, Ely, Cambridgeshire 1986. Sense of Style – Paul Hallam and Mick Mouskos, Middlesex 1984. Life After '66 – Wayne Iredale, Leicester. The Catch – Chris Hunt, Ely, Cambridgeshire 1986.

THE ALL NEW FAB AND GROOVY

REFLECTIONS

- THE TRUTH
- THE JETSET
- THE PLAYN JAYN
- THE DREAM FACTORY
- EDWIN STARR

●NO.6 ●60p

LIFE AFTER '66

THE MAN FROM
U.N.C.L.E.
ALBUM REVIEWS
SINGLES REVIEWS
BOOK REVIEWS
LETTERS
JIMMY WITHERSPOON

ISSUE 3   50p

Sense of Style

January 1984 —————————— Issue No. 1

ESSEX CLUB BREAK-UP

AFTER weeks of speculation the Regency Suite, Chadwell Heath, near Ilford, has disposed of 'Ray Patriotic' and 'Eddie Piller'.

The pair from Essex had been running the club since its conception in January '83.

The split which had been brewing for some time finally came at the end of December.

Taking over on the Friday night is Soulful Shack DJ Pete Poyton. The Suite, which was easily the most popular Friday night club looks like continuing its success as no serious competition has yet arisen.

Capital Radio

Recent attractions have included a guest spot by Capital Radio's Peter Young. Peter, who hosts the stations 'Soul Cellar' did an hour spot playing classic sounds from the mid 60's.

INSIDE THIS ISSUE

Page 2
Milan News

Page 5
In Brief

Page 6
Ska Revival

Page 11
Sounds Alive

Page 12
Directory

FOR EDDIE PILLERS VIEWS SEE PAGES 8 & 9

Sense of Style, March 1984

YOU TURNED MY BITTER INTO SUITE

THE tension was high as Eddie picked up his drink and escorted me to the corner.

We were at the first night of Eddies club at Lords in Ilford. There was no denying from Eddie that the main object of the club was to draw people away from the Regency Suite only two miles down the road at Chadwell Heath.

"I don't care if we lose money tonight. The main object is to take people away from the place. The problem tonight is the lack of mods and the number of casuals."

Tension

As Eddie spoke a glass fell off a nearby speaker. We looked at each other. The tension in the club was at quite a pitch.

"I though somebody threw that," laughed Eddie.

The tone of the music changed at this point as Ray, under pressure from the pleb majority, was forced to play disco sounds to try and calm the situation which was developing.

Piller looked shocked for a moment then laughed and took to the dancefloor imitating and parodying the local funksters.

Christmas special

He returned smiling. "I hope that lot don't think I'm serious." he said pointing to a crowd that had travelled the 30 odd mis journey with me.

"I don't care if we lose money tonight"

Christmas Special held at the Suite on Boxing Day. We'd sold advance tickets and published the times, etc. when suddenly three days before the event, the management told us that the club would run from 6-12, not 12-12.

"It wasn't me and the locals that it was going to put out but people travelling from all over the south east who would have to stand for 6 hours outside."

"Previously the manager

had been putting up the rent each xmonth and charging for barmen and this sort of thing. The Boxing Day do

was just the last nail in the coffin or the straw that broke the camels back. Anyway at the end of the night we had 260 counted in at £2 each.

Dalston

"We paid the bands and by the time the manager had taken his cut Ray and I had lost £20 each. Obviously we weren't going to accept this.

"Ray and I told him our

finding Essex (his home patch) a little difficult to work at the moment.

"As well as Lords tonight Ray worked a plane last night (Thursday 12 January). Again the place was full of casuals and the manager refused admittance without a ticket. We won't go back."

'They Don't Make Them Like You Anymore', which is their own composition, or the classic Shake A Tall Feather. Aside from that they will be playing a couple of London dates before going off to Italy in March.

The trip he was speaking of was to an international mod festival. Eddie had appeared in Milan recently and I asked him how the Italian scene was.

"I enjoyed DeeJaying over there. The kids were

feelings and he told us that if we felt this way then don't bother doing it.

Eddie appears to be

the end of January.

"I've also got a late night lined up possibly on Saturdays but I can't say anymore at the moment."

As he had mentioned them I decided to bring up the point of Fast Eddie, who Piller manages.

"Early in February they should have a new single out which will be either

very smart and wearing good shoes and cardigans but no suits.

"The reason for this is the price. There are very few tailors and they are very expensive.

"When I went, the organisers asked me to play mainly northern which I don't personally like, but its what I was asked to play. Anyway I started off playing with very little response from the audience. On the spur of the moment I decided to play some classics and everybody started dancing."

Fast Eddie

"I'm going back in March with Terry Class and 30-40 others. Fast Eddie are live over there so I'm going in my managerial capacity. I might even get up and play sax with them."

The Essex entrepreneur who recently left MCA Records where he worked as a promoter has now opened a market stall.

"It was the drummer in my bands idea. Aaron asked me to help him out so I'm now a partner in this stall at Kensington Market. It caters mainly for Jazz but I recommend it to everybody."

"I hope people do go to Eddie's club's and market stall, this way he might be able to pay for his crash repairs that seem to be mounting up — Ed.

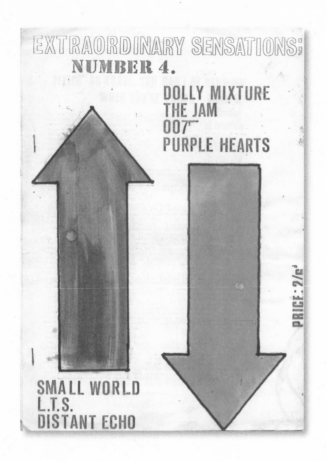

EXTRAORDINARY SENSATIONS;
NUMBER 4.

DOLLY MIXTURE
THE JAM
007
PURPLE HEARTS

PRICE: 7/6ᵈ

SMALL WORLD
L.T.S.
DISTANT ECHO

ISSUE 10
25p

SHAKE

WHAAM!

THE JAM (INTERVIEW)
THE NIP'S . THE PURPLE HEARTS

EXTRAORDINARY SENSATIONS;
NUMBER 4. P.S THE MODELS HAVE SIGNED TO STIFF

40 pence...

vespa

SMALL WORLD
L.T.S.
DISTANT ECHO

sounds

Made vs. The World

THE ONLOOKERS + CELEBRATE THE WEDDING IN STYLE!!

MEMORIES ?

TEEN BEATS

DOLLY MIXTURE
THE JAM
007
PURPLE HEARTS

MAXIMUM   No 8

SPEED

Purple Hearts

MILLIONS LIKE US / BEAT THAT !!
FICS 003

BACK TO ZERO

YOUR SIDE OF HEAVEN / BACK TO BACK
FICS 004

The Chords

BACK TO ZERO
YOUR SIDE OF HEAVEN

The Chords

NOW ITS GONE
b/w DON'T GO BACK
2059 141

and Ray Margetson being kicked out of the Regency.* It was completely different from what anyone else was writing about."

And then there were the covers. The lack of colour photocopiers in the late seventies and early eighties made a full-colour front cover something of a Holy Grail and editors often went to ridiculous lengths to feature a splash of something other than black and white.

Dominic Kenny's **Shake** was one of the first modzines to come up with a colour front cover, which included a pop art line drawing of Paul Weller with yellow and red flashes. Early modzine **Direction Reaction Creation** concentrated on front covers that managed to somehow look professional while retaining the integrity and charm of a home-made production line.

For Issue 4 of **Extraordinary Sensations**, I had decided to produce a limited number of copies that featured an exclusive design on the front cover, in addition to the standard cut-and-paste collage. I had no idea how to go about this, but as the eighties progressed, the number of fanzines was multiplying at an exponential rate and there was growing competition for rack space at Robot, so I wanted **ES** to stand out from the crowd.

In the end, I printed a number of plain covers with a pair of plain white arrows with a thick black border, one pointing up and one pointing down. I then cut out a chunky card stencil and purchased bottles of red and blue ink from an art shop. I dipped lumps of cotton wool into the ink and rubbed the sopping blobs within the confines of the stencil. The result was a rather amateurish red and blue 'pop art' edition. I'd got the idea from Ed Ball and Dan Treacy's Whaam! record label, as they'd been releasing records with hand-painted sleeves.

It took an incredible amount of effort to produce even a small amount of hand-coloured covers, meaning it was an experiment that I did not repeat; after I'd made 50 of the red and blue ones, I reverted to a collage that featured a photo of a young Andrew Loog Oldham.**

In the end, we hit on a different idea: why not persuade an advertiser to pay for a full-colour print job?

Goffa Gladding remembers: "People were genuinely in shock about the colour cover. Honestly, even though we eventually decided to go ahead with it, we absolutely agonised about whether we should take the corporate dollar. Even more so, we couldn't really agree on the kind of cover that we were actually agreeing to have paid for by Polydor. I mean, it was an advert, just a bloody advert. But in the end, we just thought it was too great an opportunity to miss. It was just before the March of the Mods tour, which was the biggest non-Jam event of our scene up to that point."

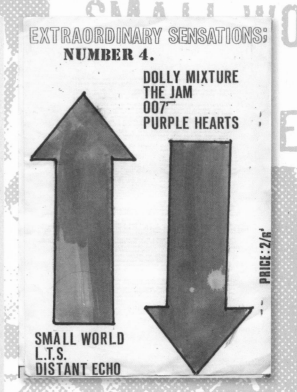

EXTRAORDINARY SENSATIONS:
NUMBER 4.

DOLLY MIXTURE
THE JAM
007
PURPLE HEARTS

PRICE: 2/6'

SMALL WORLD
L.T.S.
DISTANT ECHO

Extraordinary Sensations Eddie Piller and Terry Rawlings, Essex 1981. **Shake** – Dom Kenny and Mike. **Maximum Speed** – Goffa Gladding, Clive Reams and Kim Gault, London 1979.

*I had been running a highly successful mod club at the Regency Suite with Ray 'Patriotic' Margetson and a number of other DJs. It was held twice a week for three years and was extremely successful, even featuring in a BBC documentary. We felt that the club's owner resented the fact that he had to pay us, and we were one day unceremoniously dumped and replaced by him... only for the night to fold a couple of months later!

**Andrew Loog Oldham was manager of The Rolling Stones from 1963 to 1967 and established the extremely exciting Immediate label, whose byline was 'Proud To Be Part Of The Industry Of Human Happiness'.

Sadly, the tour didn't go happily, but the mod revival continued unabashed. Ray Margetson, editor of *Patriotic*, also invested his own money in a number of limited edition colour cover splashes, most notably including the Union Jack.

"It was a bit of a nuisance actually, as we had to print a whole A3 page on glossy paper (the fanzine being A4 and A3 being twice the size), which had the front and back covers as well as the inside cover pages. It cost quite a bit more and the printer had to wrap it round the rest of the fanzine rather like a sleeve. The end result was worth it, though."

Kev Bagnall from the South London-based fanzine *XL5* often printed his front covers on a bold-coloured background, like yellow or blue, with one-colour black print, again to stand out on the racks at Robot.

Kev tells his story: "*XL5* first made an appearance in February 1981 and I produced a total of four issues over a 12-month period. In general, it was completely ink-splattered and produced on an old Rotopress drum-based copier, which meant that the photos were crap and you couldn't even read bits of it, but at least the words were good! It was actually my second attempt at a fanzine, following the poor attempt that was *See You In Court*, which I typed and wrote onto yellow paper, meaning that when it photocopied you couldn't read anything! I had always wanted to write (and I still write, as an unpublished author) and avidly read all the fanzines I could get my hands on wishing I could do it. So I did.

"I was good friends with Steve Roadrunner and he influenced me a lot, along with reading *Beat Crazy*, *Clever Remarks*, *Jamming!* and *Extraordinary Sensations*. Primarily, I wanted to feature bands that other fanzines and certainly the national music press didn't, but I started Issue 1 with a long interview with Long Tall Shorty, during the time Derwent Jaconelli and Marcus Vandell joined the line-up. Myself and my brother, Neil, were big fans of the band and eventually became good friends with Derwent and their leader Tony Perfect, just by following them around. We also featured a band called Modern Jazz, who were very different from the others on the mod scene at the time (and may well have become Mood 6 later on?), although their article printed very badly. Other bands we covered included Dolly Mixture and The Gymslips.

"I wanted the fanzine to be more than interview/review/interview/review so later issues had other bits in there too. I stopped because in early '82 I found myself more and more involved as a musician with the band Apocalypse, so I had no real time to devote to *XL5*. Moreover, the scene itself was dissipating and splitting into psychedelia and jazz, and although I liked both, many people didn't, and there were other bands that needed to be featured, such as The Alarm, The Mood Elevators, Ok Jive, Garage, The Rainbow Remiped Dance Band and Rudi, none of whom fit into that scene at all.

XL5 — Kev Bagnall, London 1981.
Clever Remarks — Mark & Mike, London 1981.
Patriotic — Ray Margetson, London 1982.

"Also, I saw other fanzines getting better and better with production and I wanted to produce something that was much better too. I actually left it for about a year or so, got a job at an ad agency where I could produce more, and then wrote one issue each of *Rhythm Plus* (featuring an interview with Paul Hardcastle,* during which he played me a demo of his enormous hit '19') and *Strong Foundation* (featuring interviews with Latin Quarter, 52nd Street and Curiosity Killed The Cat), before I finally retired from fanzinery. The gig scene had gone too much into DJ'ing and sampling for me, and I found myself harking back to the older days rather than seeking out new music, which I thought was getting a bit samey. Fanzines are like a bug, they can get under your skin…"

*Paul Hardcastle is a British smooth jazz/synthpop/electro house composer, musician and producer, whose song '19' went to number one in the UK in 1985.

Kickstart — Thomas Stafford, Dublin 1992/1993.
Circles — Ralph, Waltham Cross 1985.
Over Under Sideways Down.
Sawdust Caesars — Dave Edwards, London 1992/1994.

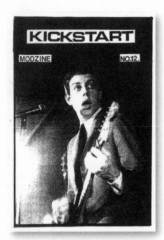

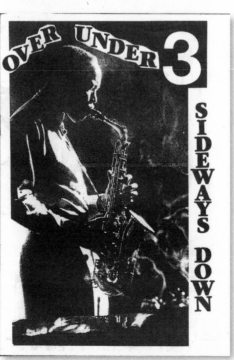

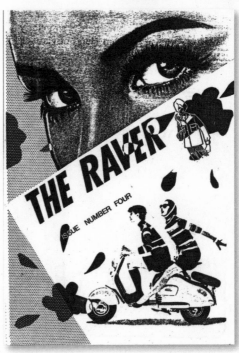

The Raver — Paul 'Smiler' Anderson,
Reading 1989.
The New Stylist — R Paddison, Leeds 1983.

'THE BRITISH WAY OF LIFE':

REGIONAL MOD ZINES

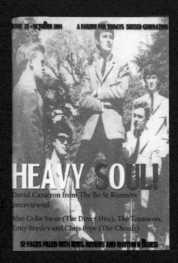

Right Track — Jim Watson and Garry Moore, Essex 1981/1986.
Face to Face — Kev Morgans (RIP) and Andy Oakley, Derbyshire 1983/1987.
Heavy Soul! — Adam Cooper, Winslow, Bucks 2010/ongoing.
Then Now Always — Tony Clark, Warren Bright and Joe Average, Essex 1983/1986.

IMMEDIATE

As the second wave of the mod revival spread throughout the country, regional fanzines assumed ever-greater importance. Editors tended to become DJs or promoters and consequently drove the underground scene in their own regions.

The Bull brothers, Andy and Jud, were early subscribers to *Extraordinary Sensations*. They described their home town of Chesterfield, Derbyshire, as a hotbed of fanzine activity.

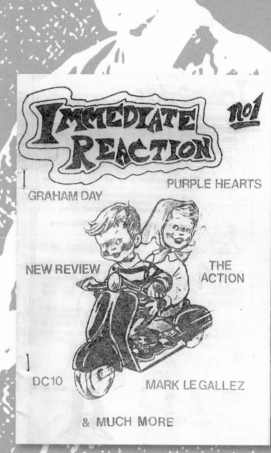

Andy remembers: "The one myself and our Jud ran was *Immediate Reaction*. The first issue came out on January 30, 1985 (accidentally on Steve Marriott's birthday), and ran for 13 issues until the spring of 1992. The last three issues actually sold more copies in France and Australia than the UK. Chesterfield and the surrounding area had quite a few fanzines, but the longest-running were ours and *Face To Face*, which was put together by Kev Morgans, who sadly passed away in 2017 aged just 51. We also had the short-lived *Suedehead Times*, which was actually edited by my nephew, Tony Smith.

"The brilliant thing about being a fanzine editor was that we travelled all over the country and met hundreds of people we didn't know who became instant friends. In 1984, when I was 16, we came down to the Ilford Palais all-dayer and London's 100 Club to see Purple Hearts. After spending the previous two or three years reading all about the London scene in other people's fanzines, actually going there was a real eye-opener and a great starting point for putting our own zine together. Sometimes the scene could be really cliquey. I can remember we really upset a lot of people, especially Mark Johnson from *The Phoenix List*, for doing a rather detailed article on Bank Holiday violence in Issue 4 and then following it up with a piece on skinhead fanzines in number 5!"

Another long-running Derbyshire fanzine was Gaz Poundall's *What's Happening Today!*, based in Spondon.

"I did the first two issues with Mick Shaw and then carried on on my own. We did eight issues in total and the experience I gained with the zine led me to promote my own gigs with some of the bigger scene bands of the time, people like Makin' Time, The Scene and The Rage. I mainly concentrated on bands from the '79 revival and onwards. I know many fanzines covered the sixties but there were enough people doing that, so I left it alone. The fanzine also published a few cassette tapes of new bands and also an international one called *United*, which I compiled with a Danish fanzine editor called Karsten Rene Hee – it featured British bands on side one and a collection of overseas groups on side two. It was pretty successful at the time."

Over in Rushden, Northamptonshire, Jim McAlwane and Kev Byfield ran the successful *First Impressions* fanzine while they were still at school.

FACE TO FACE
modzine

Issue..11   30p.

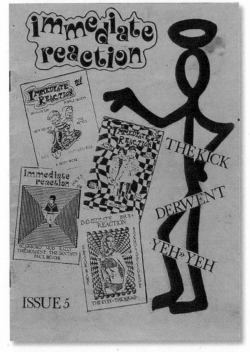

Face to Face – Kev Morgans (RIP) and Andy
Oakley, Derbyshire 1985/1987.
Immediate Reaction – Andy Bull, Chesterfield
1985/1992.
What's Happening Today – Gaz Poundall,
Derbyshire 1983.

whats
happening
today

issue three
Limited Edition

DECEMBER 83

WHATS
HAPPENING
TODAY!

45p

issue five

The Blades
The Crowd
Episode 3
First Impressions
Geno Vess
New Review

The Pride
The Scene
The Way Out

AND OTHER
VARIOUS ARTICLES

WHAT'S
HAPPENING
TODAY!

Issue 6

50p

CONTENTS INCLUDE:

Blues Brothers
Buddy Ascott
Male Fashion
Plenty of Band Info.

WHAT'S
HAPPENING
TODAY!   7.

What's Happening Today — Gaz Poundall
Derbyshire 1983/1986.
Immediate Reaction — Andy Bull,
Chesterfield 1985/1992.

Jim McAlwane: "We made seven issues in total; the first couple shipped around 200 to 250, but from then on we became more popular and were selling more than 500. By the time of Issue 5, Kev went off to start his own fanzine, which was called *Look Sharp*, while I continued the last three on my own, finally shutting up shop in '85.

"The Northamptonshire mod scene was quite large, with scooters and events everywhere. Writing the fanzine made me many friends. Kev and I went down to London every week to watch bands and generally hang about down Carnaby Street. We travelled down to the record shops in Camden Town and Portobello Road, which also had a healthy selection of fanzines for sale. Another great memory was the first gig, October 25, 1984 – The Scene, Direct Hits and The Way Out at the 100 Club; we were so excited, Kev bunked off school to watch it and I had only just left."

Further south, Essex had always been one of the main centres for the mod scene and was consequently home to a large number of fanzines. One of the more professional efforts was *Right Track*, edited by Jim Watson and Garry Moore.

Jim recalls: "The first fanzine I ever read was *Maximum Speed*, which I picked up outside a Jam gig in '79. It was a light-bulb moment for me and made me think I could produce something like it. I didn't act on the impulse for a few years but I eventually created *Right Track* with Letraset and my nan's old typewriter. After the second issue, I was running out of ideas, so Garry came on board as co-editor and brought some great ideas and limitless enthusiasm. Together we perfected what became our trademark style: biting sarcasm blended with observations on the scene and copious reviews. My personal interest was very firmly in the rhythm and soul scene, and I was lucky enough to have Ian Clark, the Kent Records sleeve designer, send me images, while Ady Croasdell [boss of Kent and founder of the 6T's Soul Club] sent me many of his releases to review. Pages were still hand-typed, though, and often adorned with poor-quality photos from a Kodak 110 – it was all tremendously difficult compared to the technology that is available today."

His co-editor, Garry, continues: "I used to buy *Sounds*, *Melody Maker* and the *NME* when I was at school, but they were just too general. However, fanzines were a much more interesting prospect, being focused on specific topics, and the mod scene represented a state of attitude and a rebellious set of values that I found alluring. I found that mod fanzines set out to capture and portray this lifestyle with articles I was really interested in, current bands I wanted to see, bands from the sixties I was interested in, fashion, scooters and, most importantly, reviews of clubs and scooter rallies and where we should go to meet like-minded people, which was extremely important in those pre-social media days.

First Impressions – Jim McAlwane and Kev Byfield,
Rushden, Northants 1984.
Look Sharp – Kev Byfield Rushden, Northants 1985.
Right Track – Jim Watson and Garry Moore,
Essex 1985.

ISSUE 2

LOOK²
SHARP

mödzine

Interviews
with.
THE MOMENT!
the combine.
THE GENTS.
SOLID STATE & THE GENTS
gig review.

THE THEME
the cigarettes.
THE BLADES.   SEVENTEEN
                   17
the risk.
the rage.   PLUS
                   STAX
                   MORE.

FIRST IMPRESSIONS

PLUS EXCLUSIVE Episode 3 INTERVIEW-ETTE

Modzine

NUMBER 3 FEATURES

THE SCENE

THE **'COMBINE'**

The **DIRECT HITS**

DEE ★ WALKER

The **MOMENT**

AND SPACKS MORE INSIDE..!

Get Ready For →

«PLUS new **HEIGHTS** INTERVIEW»

FIRST IMPRESSIONS

Modzine

The Gents INTERVIEW
Mark Le Gallez
Prisoners

and tons more inside— 👉

No.4

The Scene
GIG REVIEW..!

plus-
**THE '79 BANDS
THAT GOT AWAY**

17

and Reviews, X-Word, Pix, Des the Mod etc.
→ → →

MODZINE FIRST no.5

IMPRESSIONS

FEATURING→ Colliding circleS, STAPREST,
THE GENTS, THE MOMENT, RAGE,
THE THEME, FASHION, X-WORD,
ELEANOR RIGBY, GIG REVIEWS + MORE.
THE SQUAD,

Look Sharp - Kev Byfield, Rushden,
Northants 1985.
First Impressions - Jim McAlwane and
Kev Byfield, Rushden, Northants 1984.

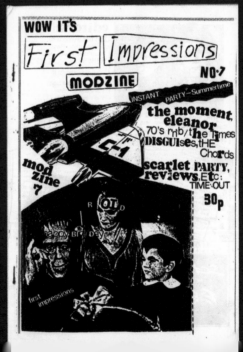

WOW ITS

First Impressions

MODZINE

NO.7

INSTANT PARTY—Summertime

the moment, eleanor
70's rnb/the Times
DISGUISes, tHE Chords
**scarlet PARTY,
reviews** Etc:
TIME OUT

mod zine 7

30p

first impressions

First
№ 6

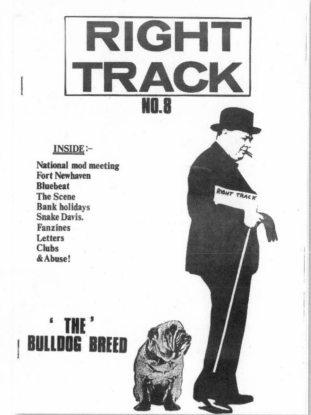

Right Track – Jim Watson and
Garry Moore, Essex 1981/1986.

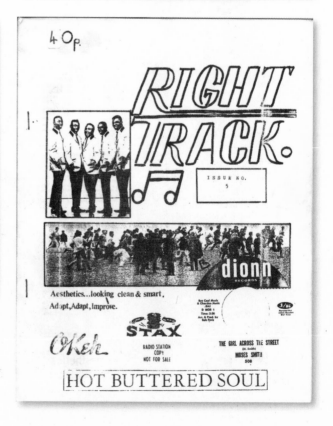

RIGHT TRACK NO.10

FREE GIFT INSIDE!
Plus
Modern Jazz
Bank Hols.
Ad Libs
R&B Index Pt.2
Makin' Time
        Interview
And More.

NLG 680C

Kaleidoscope One

* INside: Brighton Who Gig,

KLIOCP AEDSOE

Plus, The
Hearts At The
Bridgehouse

Kinks, l to r: Mick Avory, Peter Quaife,
Ray Davies, Dave Davies.

"*Right Track* was one of my favourites. I picked it up at the Greyhound in Chadwell Heath. I got to know Jim and he asked me to write a review of the 1981 scooter run to Margate, as he told me that getting enough material to fill the whole fanzine was always a problem. Jim liked the piece and ended up asking me to get on board as co-editor.

"As we moved through into the mid-eighties, the mod scene went further underground, becoming more style- and values-driven in the process. Tolerance to non-core influences like casuals and scooter boys shrunk, and *Right Track* became a champion of those early mod ideals by heavily promoting its early R&B influences, mod-only clubs and rallies, sharp sixties fashion and the original classic car movement – all injected with our own brand of humour and abuse. We were young and I guess we just didn't care about anyone else – that was what it was all about for us."

Fanzines were essential to sharing the new trends appearing on the mod scene. Epping, also in Essex, was home to the short-lived title *Kaleidoscope*. The Sylvester brothers, Ed and John, had both become mods at the very beginning of 1979 and were extremely passionate. By 1981, the mod scene had broadened somewhat to take in the burgeoning psych scene, which featured a crossover of mod/psych bands like The Playn Jayn, Mood Six, Doctor & The Medics, Bees By Post and Le Mat. This mod revival offshoot also had its own, more psychedelic-influenced clothes shops, like Sweet Charity and the Regal and a superbly successful club in Piccadilly called the Groovy Cellar.*

Ed Silvester continues: "There seemed to be loads of fanzines popping up in the summer of '81 and ours was a bit of a one-hit wonder, mainly about the emerging psych scene – we sold around 300 copies and we used the same printer as *Extraordinary Sensations* at the time, Dave Stokes. This was because he was the only one we knew in the print game and he was local! We had a rather belligerent piece on Small World, which was written by local face Michael Spencer, and rather unsurprisingly I remember having to substantially edit it! I also remember we crammed in some bits from our local paper when one of the Epping mods, Smiffy, had an unfortunate, but relatively amusing, looking back-brush with the law. We pretty much sold out the whole print run in just one night at the Phoenix Club in New Cavendish Square at a Tony Class night. We did have loads of other stuff that we could have used for Issue 2 but we kinda ran out of time and lost interest in the end. I reckoned that, by their very nature, fanzines were instantly disposable and very much of their time."

Lack of time seems to be the main reasons fanzine editors let their magazines just fade away.

In Chris Hunt's case, "I stopped producing *Shadows And Reflections* because it just felt like it was time for the fanzine to come to an end, but also because I was starting to write for national magazines. I was the original

Hayling Island, Clyde McPhatter, Modern Jazz, News & Views....

*Incidentally, this offshoot scene was well documented at the time in the quasi-documentary *The Groovy Movie*, which has now surfaced on YouTube and provides an interesting snapshot of a rather quirky side to the mod revival.

music columnist for **Scootering** and was writing articles for Dave
Henderson's **Underground** and the weekly music paper **Record Mirror**,
plus I was about to take on the job of editing a specialist national magazine,
Hip-Hop Connection.* What it actually meant was that if there was a band
I really wanted to write about, whether it was The Moment, the James Taylor
Quartet, or Boys Wonder, I could do it for a wider audience."

While it was only just starting for many, it was ending for some. Terry Rawlings
remembers the final days of **Extraordinary Sensations**.

"To be honest, after Issue 14, me and Eddie had just had enough. We were
getting a hundred letters every week and had just lost our office. It was a room
above an East London haulage operation in Dagenham and Ernie Brain, the
guy who had given us the space for three years gratis, wanted to sell up and
redevelop the yard. We didn't really mind but, as so often happens, things
come along and directions change.

"Paul Weller, who was so extraordinarily supportive of the fanzine when it was
at its peak, suggested we move into his office suite in London and so we did.
It was so very professional. We had been used to rocking up at lunchtime and
putting on a John Lee Hooker LP for an hour and then popping down the pub.
Paul disciplined us and made us take it seriously. I never really worked out why
Paul Weller backed the mod fanzine world as much as he did, but there was
no doubt that he dragged us forward. The last two issues of **ES** would never
have come out if it hadn't been for him. It was like we were just part of the
same gang of old mods. Talking and arguing about what mod actually was.
Truth be told, I don't think Paul has changed. He was always more obsessed
with mod fanzines than I was."

When Stiff Records came calling with the option to run a mod label,
Extraordinary Sensations was soon shelved and myself, Rawlings and
Maxine Conroy walked away to start Countdown Records.

But the world of mod fanzines carried on without us, new titles continuing
to appear everywhere.

That hotbed of 1980s modernism, Northern Ireland, was especially bristling
with new zines. At its peak, **Extraordinary Sensations** had around 350 direct
subscribers in the province alone, who would send in their pound notes in
envelopes decorated with targets – some red, white and blue, others green,
white and orange, depending on which particular community they hailed from,
but it was always good-natured. The mod scene was almost totally blind to the
rest of the sectarian pressures that were rife in the province.

Terry Rawlings again: "It was extraordinary; as well as the subscribers, we
would send around 500 copies of each new issue over to Caroline Music in
Belfast and they would sell out within a couple of weeks and be on the phone
for more!"

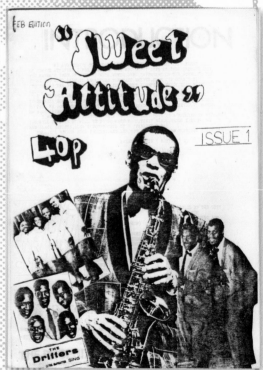

Keep The Faith – Don Clarke, Newtownabbey,
N Ireland 1983.
Sweet Attitude – Arleen Slevin, Belfast,
N Ireland 1985.
Faraway Voices – Tony Arnold and Mark
Lavery, Belfast, N Ireland 1983.
Trans-Global Express – Phil Snowdon and
John McAleer, Newtownabbey, N Ireland 1983.

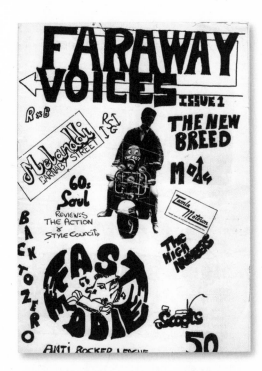

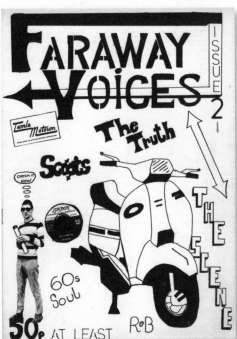

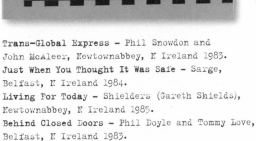

Trans-Global Express – Phil Snowdon and
John McAleer, Newtownabbey, N Ireland 1983.
Just When You Thought It Was Safe – Sarge,
Belfast, N Ireland 1984.
Living For Today – Shielders (Gareth Shields),
Newtownabbey, N Ireland 1985.
Behind Closed Doors – Phil Doyle and Tommy Love,
Belfast, N Ireland 1983.
For Now And Forever – Sean McKee, Antrim,
N Ireland 1984.

On The Four Winds – Johnny Hamilton, Gary
Weir and Steven Hughes, Carrickfergus
N Ireland 1984. Happening Right Now – Johnny
Hamilton, Carrickfergus, N Ireland 1984.
Kick In The Head – Johnny Hamilton
Carrickfergus, N Ireland 1990.
Smarter Than U! – Jake Lingwood, Kent 1986/1987.
Psychotic Reaction – David Holmes, Belfast
N Ireland 1985. In The City – Stuart Currie,
Belfast, N Ireland 1982.
In The Crowd – Derek 'Delboy' Shepherd,
Guernsey, 1984.

Roger Dixon remembers the Saturday ritual in Belfast. "Many of the young mods would congregate in Lower Garfield Street in the city centre and check out the latest fanzine imports and records. The big ones were *Extraordinary Sensations*, *Roadrunner* and *Patriotic*. We also had quite a few of our own. Homer produced one called *Psychotic Reaction* and we had *In The City* and *Get Ready*… literally dozens more too."

Once the fanzine bug bites, it can last a lifetime. Belfast's Jonny Hamilton published no fewer than four different titles between 1983 and 2010.

"Like many others at the time, I had been inspired to give it a go after I saw a piece on *The Tube* TV show on fanzines and then picked up a copy of *Extraordinary Sensations* at Caroline Music. I thought it looked easy enough. I edited my first two, *On The Four Winds* and *Happenin' Right Now*, in '83 and '84. Then I had a break for five years and came back with four issues of a new title, *Kick In The Head*, and finally in 2010 I edited two issues of *One Two Five*. The fanzine bug never really left me…"

Back in England, *Smarter Than U* was a fanzine from Kent that bristled with, as its title suggests and Jake Lingwood succinctly puts it, "sharp arrogance and evil wit". It ran in the mid-to late eighties and was established by Jake, now a senior executive at the publishing company Random House/ Penguin.

"Even though we had short production runs, starting at 50 for the first and 150 for the third and final issue, the editorial standards were comparatively very high. It looked strong, too. Pure mod. Although we were from Herne Bay, I would regard the fanzine as very much 'national', as we sold it at mod rallies and gigs. You can even see me flogging it to the queue at the famous Purple Hearts all-dayer at the Hippodrome on some archaic TV documentary! The whole experience later helped me get into publishing, as I'd pretty much worked it all out myself already!"

Probably the most successful and prolific fanzine of the lot was *In The Crowd*, which stretched to an extraordinary 30 issues. Based in the tiny Channel Island of Guernsey, it was the creation of Derek Shepherd (and his long-term partner, Jackie) who often went by the name of 'Delboy'. Here he explains how and why an island better known for its years of wartime occupation and, much later, being a haven for motorcycle-riding greasers became synonymous with the longest-running modzine of them all.

"Of course the mod scene in the Channel Islands was small but extremely dedicated. I would say that there were around 60 mods on Guernsey when we published the first issue of *In The Crowd* in 1983. We started because I was heartily sick of the mod scene being ignored, or worse, getting negative coverage from the mainstream press. It seemed that the mod scene was dropped after '79 and the press went on to their next plaything. We really felt that it was us against the world and wanted to self-promote our world in

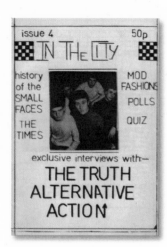

In The City — Stuart Currie,
Belfast, N Ireland 1982/1986.
Get Ready — Dee Warren and
Alan McKeag, Belfast,
N Ireland 1984.
Kick In The Head — Johnny
Hamilton, Carrickfergus,
N Ireland 1989.
125 — Johnny Hamilton,
Carrickfergus,
N Ireland 2009.

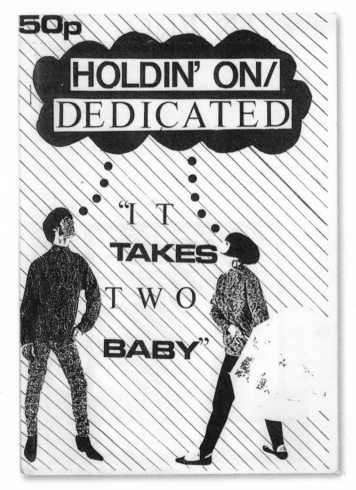

Dedicated — Steve Patterson, Craigavon,
N Ireland 1983/19855.
Holdin' On — Gerry Kavanagh and Mark
Mulholland, Co Armagh, N Ireland 1985.
Psychotic Reaction — David Holmes, Belfast
N Ireland 1984.
125 — Johnny Hamilton,
Carrickfergus, N Ireland 2011.
Holdin' On/Dedicated — Joint effort
between Steve Patterson and Mark Mulholland
Craigavon, N Ireland 1986.

a good way or die out. I remember the first modzine I started reading was **Extraordinary Sensations** and I loved finding out that there were other mods out there, what they were interested in and that we were actually part of something a whole lot bigger.

"I would say that the main problem we faced was that we were so far away from the majority of mod-related events because it was really difficult to get to the mainland. To circumvent this, we asked contributors and editors of other fanzines from around the world to submit articles and we had an extraordinary response. This made **ITC** a rather cosmopolitan modzine with a variety of views and opinion, not just our own."

An extraordinarily large amount of work would have gone into editing 30 fanzine issues in just seven years, so just how popular was **In The Crowd**?

Derek remembers: "I'm proud to say that we issued more editions than any other mod fanzine and I remember we sold less than 100 copies of our first one. By the time we had done a dozen, we were up to 2,500 [sales] every issue. I have to give credit to Bart Mendoza from the American band Manual Scan, who by that time had sorted out US distribution for us. We had also picked up a trick from **Direction Reaction Creation** and started giving away flexi-discs with every copy.

"By the late eighties things were slowing down a bit, as we had fewer outlets, and I think our last issue in 1990 only sold 1,500! Ours was very much an international publication by the end, selling everywhere there was a mod scene: the UK, Ireland, the USA, Italy, France, Holland, Belgium, Spain, Norway, Sweden, Denmark, Austria, Japan, Canada, Australia and even South America. Our main British outlet was in Carnaby Street – there were so many shops around there that stocked us: Carnaby Cavern, the Rockafella Centre (or Robot), Sherry's and Merc. I had also secured outlets in Dublin, Belfast, Birmingham, Swindon and Cardiff. We also had a few hundred direct subscribers' and once the mod societies became more established, they would all sell **In The Crowd**, which upped our circulation again.

"We actually started printing the fanzine on my co-editor Jackie's school photocopier, but we always tried to improve with every issue and often experimented with different ways to make the experience better for our readers, hence turning glossy and eventually with cover colours."

Unlike the majority of fanzines, **In The Crowd**'s editors didn't stop producing new issues because they ran out of time or commitment.

"I called time on **In The Crowd** after 30 issues because, in 1989, Jackie and I had moved over to the mainland and then split up as a couple in 1990. I wasn't in the right state of mind to carry on the zine without her, as it was very much our magazine. I was going to give up altogether until I went to

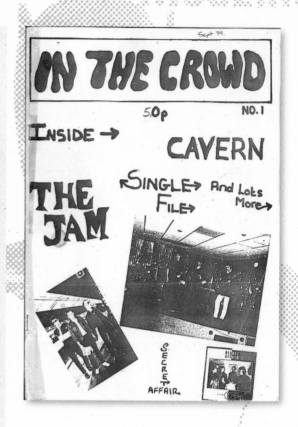

In The Crowd – Derek 'Delboy' Shepherd,
Guernsey, 1983/1990

IN THE CROWD

NO.2
INSIDE:- 40p

9 BELOW ZERO

SMALL WORLD INTERVIEW

Single File

FAST EDDIE

JAM FLEXI TO BE WON!

IN THE CROWD

No.3

INSIDE:

THE TRUTH

THE SCENE

SQUIRE

IN THE CROWD

DIRECT HITS INTERVIEW

small world

OCT 93   the Prisoners

the colours

the scene

5

IN THE CROWD

issue 7

PRISONERS INTERVIEW

GUERNSEY MOD SCENE

THE CYNICS

SMALL WORLD

THE MOMENT

IN THE CROWD

issue 8

SQUIRE & CO STARS INTERVIEW

THE NOW POWER OF

IN THE CROWD

JUNE '84   ISSUE 9

IN THE CROWD

issue 10

beat direction

dee walker

bite the bullet

Pretty things

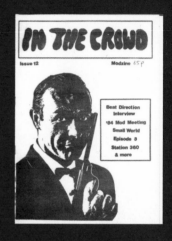

IN THE CROWD

Issue 12   Modzine 65p

Beat Direction Interview

'84 Mod Meeting
Small World
Episode 3
Station 360
& more

IN THE CROWD

NUMBER 13   MODZINE

IN THE CROWD

ISSUE 15   MODZINE

Flexi Inside

IN THE CROWD

MODZINE   £1.00   NO. 20

FLEXI SINGLES

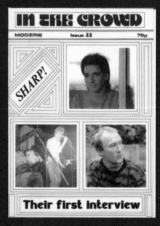

IN THE CROWD

MODZINE   Issue 22   75p

SHARP!

Their first interview

In The Crowd
Derek 'Delboy' Shepherd,
Guernsey, 1983/1990.

IN THE CROWD
MODZINE   ISSUE 25   75p

IN THE CROWD
MODZINE
ISSUE 27
80p

1979 SPECIAL-Part 2

IN THE CROWD
ISSUE 28   80p   MODZINE

'79 - '89 - STILL GOING STRONG.

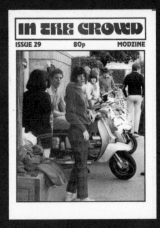

IN THE CROWD
ISSUE 29   80p   MODZINE

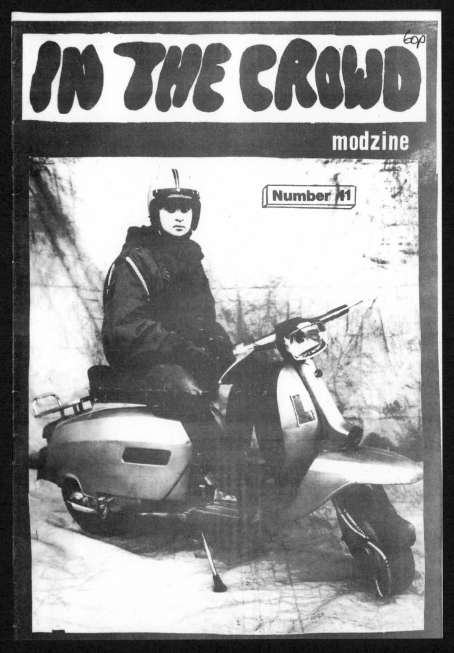

60p

IN THE CROWD
modzine

Number 11

IN THE CROWD
MODZINE   75p   ISSUE 21

FOR THE HIP AND DEDICATED MOD!

IN THE CROWD

MODZINE
ISSUE 23
£1.00

NCC-1701

THE OFFBEATS
"OR THE MILLIONTH TIME"

FLEXI DISC

"DOWN MY STREET"
THE PICTURES

"WITH THIS ISSUE"

In The Crowd – Derek 'Delboy' Shepherd,
Guernsey, 1983/1990.

a mod rally on the Isle of Wight and realised how much I actually missed doing a modzine. That's when I decided to start afresh and went back to basics with a new one called *Tailor Made*. We did nine issues until 1998, when it just became too much to carry on with and sell after Britpop died off."

Derek Shepherd's legacy of 39 in-depth issues over 15 years will probably never be beaten.

"There may have been better written and better laid-out modzines than ours, but for our sheer dedication you could not beat us really. In the end, I think fanzines just went out of fashion; for me it was a decreasing number of shops who stocked them for us, a declining readership, and of course the internet after that. I am proud that we did our part and helped keep the mod scene alive through some dark times in the late eighties and kept the flag flying in the nineties so that there was still a scene for people to rediscover or find anew. It wasn't until very recently, through speaking to people on Facebook, that I understand how much getting a copy of *In The Crowd* meant to them and made them feel part of the scene, even when they were the only mod in their town. Makes me feel proud of the fact that people have such fond memories of us and the modzine, and still have an appreciation of what we did for the scene."

Guernsey was far from the only holiday destination to host its own modzine. Tony Clark, along with Warren Bright and Howard Joe Average, edited two different titles out of the Essex village Clacton-on-Sea for three years from 1983. They released six issues of *Then, Now and Always*, while Tony also released four issues of *Sounds Exciting*.

Tony recalls: "We put on a lot of events at the Westcliff Hotel and they ran on both Friday and Saturday nights for well over four years. All the major bands played there, and groups like Solid State, The Moment, Small World and Fast Eddie made it their second home. People came from all over the country, so it was easy to shift the fanzines at the events. I think *Time Out* magazine even named us 'Best Mod Club in the Country', which made me really proud.

"I got the bug when I picked up a copy of *Maximum Speed* at an early gig by Secret Affair and The Mods, and decided to have a go. Dave Stokes from Epping was really important, as he became the main printer for Essex modzines, and as we used to shift around 800 copies a go, the fact that he was really easy to work with made it all possible. Our fanzines really reflected the whole mod vibe of our town. We were very close to the East London scene, too. Working with the guys was great fun, and the fanzines and the Westcliff Hotel made me friends for life…"

Jamie McGreal also edited a fanzine from a seaside town, this time on the south coast.

RALLIES, BANDS, RECORDS, & FANZINES, ALL REVIEWED IN YOUR BUMPER SUMMER FUN EDITION OF T.M.

144

THEN NOW ALWAYS! NO.3

CLACTON RUN 84
THE MOMENT.
CO-STARS.

RnB

FAST EDDIE &
WIPE-OUT!
LIVE
LOTS MORE!!

PRISONERS - INTERVIEW.

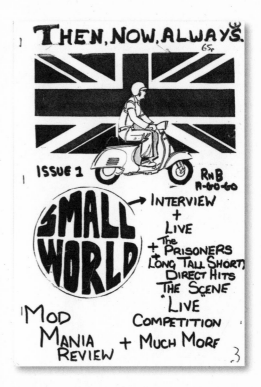

THEN, NOW, ALWAYS.
65p

ISSUE 1   RnB
R-60-60

SMALL WORLD

→ INTERVIEW
+
LIVE
The PRISONERS
+ LONG TALL SHORTY
DIRECT HITS
THE SCENE
*LIVE
COMPETITION
+ MUCH MORE

MOD MANIA REVIEW

3

SOUNDS EXCITING!   no.4   60p

INSIDE:

The Moment.
1979 revisited.
The Prisoners.
The Teisel
Interview.
&
lots more!

THE SCENE CONFESS

Tailor Made – Derek 'Delboy'
Shepherd, Wiltsure, 1983/1990.
Then Now Always – Tony Clark,
Warren Bright and Joe Average,
Essex 1983/1986.
Sounds Exciting – Tony Clark,
Essex 1985.

THEN NOW ALWAYS! no.4

THE COLOURS   INSIDE   DIRECT HITS!
SMALL WORLD   + MUCH MORE.
Prisoners   TRUTH

Tailor Made – Derek Shepherd, Chippenham 1991/1007.
Sharp! – Rob Whitmore, Glenn Ludlow, Emma Cox,
Cheltenham 1991.
The New Breed – Paul Welsby / Neil Henderson,
North West – 1999/2000.

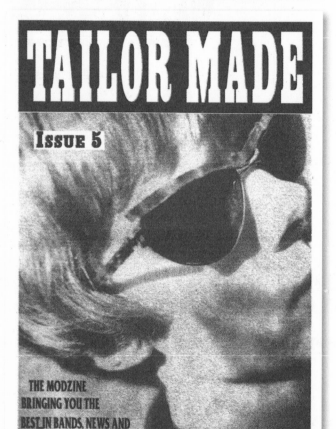

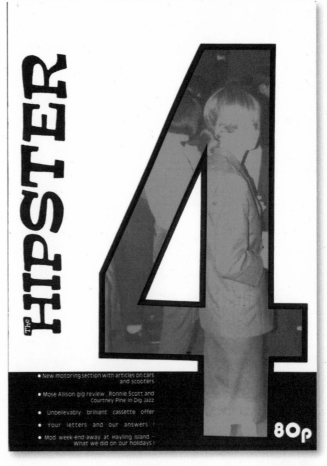

All Our Yesterdays – Mark 'Bazza' Barrett,
Middlesbrough 1993/1996.
The Hipster – Andy Clarke, Coventry 1985/1986.

"*StaRt!* was based in Bognor Regis but also had a London feel about it, as I was going there two or three times a month at the time. It only ran for two issues: we sold about 100 of the first issue and around 200 of the second. The first one came out late 1981, the second in '82. Although I only published two issues of *StaRt!*, Ray Margetson at *Patriotic* gave it a great review, and from that I had lots of postal orders from Ireland, Scotland and quite a few from Belgian mods.

"There is no doubt that, for me, writing a modzine was the highlight of this amazing period of my life and having it stocked in the Rockafella Centre in Carnaby Street was a proud moment. I was only 15 at the time, thought I was the business, and my mission was to speak my mind on how our scene should be on the south coast – unfortunately, older mods didn't see it that way! After a few controversial articles in which I was preaching the virtues of northern soul over sixties beat bands, and criticising certain dress codes, life became difficult, as I became public enemy number one! Never mind; it was a great learning curve and it was a wonderful time!"

Helen Barrell, now a successful historical true crime author, was one of a new breed of fanzine editors who took up the mantle in the nineties. In 1996, at the age of 17, she established her own fanzine while living on the Isle of Wight.

"*Dansette* ran for eight issues, two per year for four years from 1996 to 2000. The first six issues were A5 black and white and the last two were A4 with colour covers. Either Issue 7 or 8 was *Record Collector* Fanzine of the Month – I was so proud of that!

"I'd read other people's fanzines, and even wrote for one called *It's A Question Of Taste*. I realised that I could produce my own – it seemed like a good way to get in touch with people who had similar tastes, as well as being a fun thing to do. Being sent free records to review was an added bonus! Only once did I get to interview a band in person who'd been on *Top Of The Pops*, and the singer was rather rude to me. As the issues went by, *Dansette*'s focus went from indie/mod to more garage/mod, as I interviewed sixties garage punk-influenced bands via postal questionnaires, as well as Hammond organ maestro Nick Rossi and real-life sixties beat-combo star Lindsay Muir, of the band Lindsay Muir's Untamed.

"One of my favourite interviews was with Liam Watson about Toe Rag Studios, before he worked with The White Stripes.* I covered film as well as music, so I visited [film director] Josh Collins at his house in Islington, which was a converted Methodist chapel – it's where he filmed the bizarre and utterly bonkers film *Pervirella* (1997). Photographs of his prop-filled house appeared in *Dansette*'s one-and-only colour pullout section. I reviewed then-new films set in the late 1950s and 1960s, such as *The Talented Mr Ripley* (1999) and *Gangster No. 1* (2000), and wrote about collecting mid-century homewares, mod makeup, shoes and all sorts of things.

OUR EYES MET ACROSS THE CROWDED ROOM... AND SUDDENLY I KNEW ...... THIS WAS JUST THE START ......

*British record producer Liam Watson established analogue recording studio Toe Rag Studios in Shoreditch, London, in 1991, before moving to Hackney in 1997. He is perhaps best known for his work on The White Stripes' *Elephant*, which won the 2004 Grammy for Best Alternative Music Album and became one of the biggest albums of the noughties.

Start! – Jamie McGreal, Kent 1981/1982.
Dansette – Helen Barrel, Birmingham 2000.

Dansette
Helen Barrel,
Birmingham
1996/1999.

150

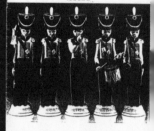

SHOOTING FROM THE HIP

MODERNIST FANZINE
ISSUE 2

INSIDE: The Byrds / The Circles / The Jolt / Maxine Brown / Ray Charles Plus much more!

Number 1

REET PETITE !

modzine

FEATURES

THE
WAY

THE
BOSS

THE
RISK

THE MERTON PARKAS

& LOTS MORE

The Charlatans - Mother Earth - Don Craine of the Downliners Sect
Corduroy - Create! - The Aardvarks - Subjagger - The Nuthins
The Creation - Martha and the Vandellas - Action Painting and more ...

Teenage Kicks – Thomas Stafford,
Dublin 1988/1990.
Shooting From The Hip – John Nelson,
Wishaw 1993.
Almost Grown – Lois Wilson, London 1995.
Reet Petite – Richard Lax,
Rotherham 1986.

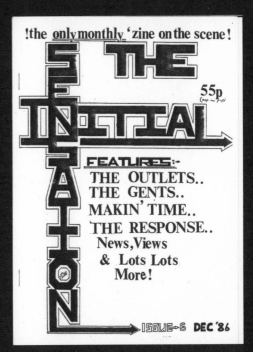

A Sixties Direction.
The Initial Sensation - Phill Bond,
Wellingborough 1986.
Shapes Of Things - Birmingham 1981.
Watcha Gonna Do About It - Rob Messer
Essex 1986.
Circles - Ralph, Waltham Cross 1985.

I even had everyone swooning with a page of male pinups in Issue 7, which featured a topless Steve McQueen. When I was 19, I used the fanzine-photocopying model of self-publishing to produce a novella called *Lament For A Trapped Spy*, which was a spy thriller set in the 1960s.

"I considered turning *Dansette* into a website, but was rather clueless about how to set one up, so by 2002 I was writing articles for the Swedish-based, English-language website Uppers.org. And by that point, poor old *Dansette* had breathed her last and the needle hissed on the run-out groove."

Adam Cooper, record label boss and editor of *Heavy Soul!*, which is both a professional mod fanzine as well as a record label, is still putting out his work every month, despite the huge amount of work that goes into producing his contemporary modzine.

"Each issue is very time-consuming. Due to family and work commitments I usually get two hours each night to sort out the label and zine. I try and start by getting the interviews targeted and researched first, as they can take the longest – each person has their own life too, so I set myself about three weeks to get it all back, and the images and the layout sorted. It's then a case of finding new tunes to write about, keeping an eye on trends, events coming up and anything interesting that might appeal through various sources. The 'classic album' section has been fun; so far we've covered albums from Makin' Time, Purple Hearts and Mother Earth. The front cover is always fun to do, too. I started by having too much on the front, but now stick to one image. There is a kind of set formula; each issue will have an editorial, news, record reviews and about six interviews. There is also a part of a story I put together serialised within. It's working out at about four to five issues per year."

While the golden years of the fanzine are over, having, like so many analogue forms of communication, been overwhelmed by the internet, blogs and social media, Adam's success shows that there's still a hunger for home-made and authentic zines.

Heavy Soul! – Adam Cooper,
Winslow, Bucks 2010/ongoing.

HEAVY SOUL!

Issue #9
October 2011

A fanzine for today's "sussed generation"

THE MISUNDERSTOOD* LOS FLECHAZOS*
THE MAGNETIC MIND*ROD SPARK*THE GET-GO
PAUL WELLER*SMALL FACES CONVENTION*THE SPITFIRES*
THE CHORDS*EDDIE PHILIPS*STONE FOUNDATION*RICHARD CASTLE*
TROJAN RECORDS*IAN SNOWBALL*CHRIS FARLOWE*BUTTON UP*DC FONTANA

52 pages filled with news, do's, reviews and Rhythm & Blues

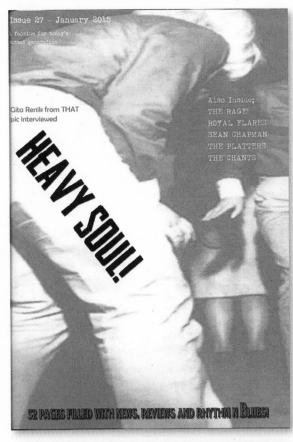

Issue 27 – January 2015

A fanzine for today's
sussed generation

Gita Renik from THAT
pic interviewed

Also Inside;
THE RAGE!
ROYAL FLARES
SEAN CHAPMAN
THE PLATTERS
THE CHANTS

HEAVY SOUL!

52 PAGES FILLED WITH NEWS, REVIEWS AND RHYTHM N BLUES!

HEAVY SOUL!....

Issue #16 January 2013

A fanzine for
today's
"sussed
generation"

52 pages filled with news, do's, reviews and Rhythm & Blues

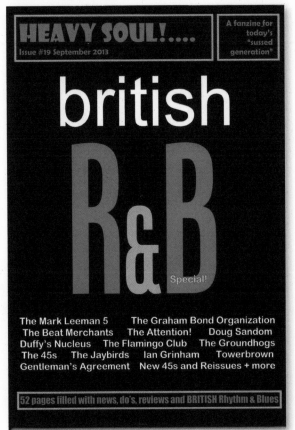

HEAVY SOUL!....

Issue #19 September 2013

A fanzine for
today's
"sussed
generation"

british

R&B
Special!

The Mark Leeman 5   The Graham Bond Organization
The Beat Merchants   The Attention!   Doug Sandom
Duffy's Nucleus   The Flamingo Club   The Groundhogs
The 45s   The Jaybirds   Ian Grinham   Towerbrown
Gentleman's Agreement   New 45s and Reissues + more

52 pages filled with news, do's, reviews and BRITISH Rhythm & Blues

Heavy Soul !....
Issue #2
September 2010

A fanzine for today's "sussed generation"

the **Galileo 7**

Featuring **Allan Crockford**   **Darrow Fletcher**
Lord Dunsby   **The Untamed**   Free 45

26 pages filled with news, do's, reviews and Rhythm & Blues !!

Heavy Soul !....
Issue #3
October 2010

A fanzine for today's "sussed generation"

WIDEBOY GENERATION

Welcome To The New Generation

Inside:
MAXINE BROWN
JIMMY SMITH

Reviewed:
THE GENTS
MOD CHRONICLES 2,
SUNLORD movie
New 45s
Reissue 45s

Classic band;
SMALL WORLD

New bands: AUNT NELLY, THE EXCITEMENTS, SMALL TALK

30 pages filled with news, do's, reviews and Rhythm & Blues

Heavy Soul !...
Issue #4
December 2010

A fanzine for today's "sussed generation"

52 pages filled with news, do's, reviews and Rhythm & Blues

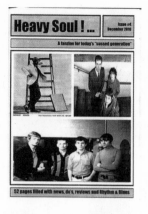

Heavy Soul !...
Issue #5
January 2011

A fanzine for today's "sussed generation"

Trevor French   *Adrian Holder*   Stone Foundation
*The Jaybirds*The Muleskinners*Towerbrown*1965 Jazz & Blues Festival
*The Electric Mess*The Small Faces*Clacton Weekender*Tommy Atkins

52 pages filled with news, do's, reviews and Rhythm & Blues

Heavy Soul!...
Issue #66
January 2012

A fanzine for today's "sussed generation"

THE STRYPES;
Beat from the Emerald Isle

JAMES TAYLOR QUARTET*MARTY McALLISTER
NICK WATERHOUSE*ROD SPARK* IRISH PAUL
PAUL MILLER*SILVER FACTORY*PEACH JANE*THE ACTION*MECCA

52 pages filled with news, do's, reviews and Rhythm & Blues

Heavy Soul !....
Issue #6
March 2011

A fanzine for today's "sussed generation"

Bob Manton*Mickey Tenner*Manual Scan

Dreamsville

52 pages filled with news, do's, reviews and Rhythm & Blues

Heavy Soul !....
Issue #7
June 2011

A fanzine for today's "sussed generation"

Baby's in black

DC FONTANA*THE meddyEVILS*CHEAP CUTS
BUTTON UP*FRANCIS JETTY*THE SCREENBEATS*THE BOGEYMEN
BEADY EYE*ARRIVAL*GREEN COOKIE RCDS*THE AFFECTED *THE CHORDS
THE UNIVERSAL*THE UPPER ↓*THE HARRINGTON BLUES*↓↓ MODZINE

52 pages filled with news, do's, reviews and Rhythm & Blues

HEAVY SOUL!
Issue #8
August 2011

A fanzine for today's "sussed generation"

NEW STREET ADVENTURE
ALEX COOPER*DEREK SHEPHERD
TERRY TONIK*THE PROFILE*
THE LAYNES*WELLER*THE WHO
WIMPLE WINCH*THE BIRDCAGE SET
THE PATTERNS*THE MYND SET*THE JAM*
VIDAL SASSOON*MICHAEL EINARUKA
EURO YE YE* IRISH JACK *TOWERBROWN
BRUTUS SHIRTS*WINDSOR JAZZ FEST 66

52 pages filled with news, do's, reviews and Rhythm & Blues

Heavy Soul!...
ISSUE #9 MARCH 2012

A FANZINE FOR TODAY'S "SUSSED GENERATION"

Paolo Hewitt

The Grenadiers
The Theme
The Reflection A.O.B.
D.C. Fontana
The Spitfires
The Hipster Image
The Prisoners
Wideboy Generation
Great Yarmouth C.C.I. '77

✦ supplement
Motown Behind The Hits?

52 pages filled with news, do's, reviews and Rhythm & Blues

Heavy Soul!...
Issue #12 May 2012

A fanzine for today's "sussed generation"

Paul
Still Relevant in 2012?
Weller

The Strypes
Tony Class
The Riots
The Afex
The Prisoners
The Ludds
The Attention!
Eric Burdon
The Eddies

52 pages filled with news, do's, reviews and Rhythm & Blues

Heavy Soul!...
Issue #13 July 2012

A fanzine for today's "sussed generation"

NOLAN PORTER

52 pages filled with news, do's, reviews and Rhythm & Blues

Heavy Soul!...
Issue #14 September 2012

A fanzine for today's "sussed generation"

52 pages filled with news, do's, reviews and Rhythm & Blues

Heavy Soul!...
Issue #15 November 2012

A fanzine for today's "sussed generation"

Inside;
ALEX
COSMETIC RECORDS
LOS SAICOS
THE VIBE CREATORS
DO THE DOG theatre
THE SPITFIRES

GRAHAM BOND
ORGANISATION
YVONNE CRAIG
THE ACTION
THE JAM
THE MOVERS

ANDY CROFTS of THE MOONS exclusive

52 pages filled with news, do's, reviews and Rhythm & Blues

Heavy Soul!....
Issue #17 April 2013

A fanzine for today's "sussed generation"

The Absolute Beginners Beginners photo album

THE JAM

HEAVY SOUL!....
Issue #19 July 2013

A fanzine for today's "sussed generation"

the universal

52 pages filled with news, do's, reviews and Rhythm & Blues

HEAVY SOUL!....
Issue #20 January 2014

A fanzine for today's "sussed generation"

Graham Day &
The Forefathers

The 45s

The Mynd Set

Speakeasy

Thee Kaams

The Travellers

The Ace

Suoke Records

The Jam

Trambeat

Paul Weller

52 pages filled with news, do's, reviews and Rhythm & Blues

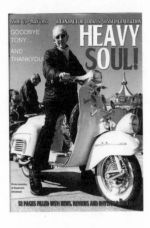

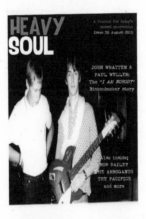

Heavy Soul! – Adam Cooper,
Winslow, Bucks 2010/ongoing.

'NEWS OF THE WORLD':

Modzines Take Many Forms

COUNTDOWN

G'day readers, Numero V is out on schedule, and is the first ish to be sent out to all those hundreds (well,dozens actually) of SUBSCRIBERS...Yes, don't forget that it's a lot easier to get your COUNTDOWN NEWS by post - all it costs is £2 for the next ten issues (first class post) or £2.50 abroad. It's also available at the NUMBER ONE CLUB THE BEN TRUEMAN and the BUSH (Sneakers) on a Sunday...From this issue, one hundred copies will be available from Jimmy at MERC in Carnaby Street as well, so you've got NO excuses not to read it, OK?...

Everybody's fave globetrotters THE UNTOUCHABLES are flying back in for their third British jaunt so far this year...It's mainly to promote their new 45 "I SPY FOR THE FBI" which is currently rising in the UK charts (59 this week)...They've got a one-off date at London's CAMDEN PALACE on the 19th of August. Tickets are available in advance for £4 but it's over eighteens only I'm afraid...You-know-who are rumoured to be supporting!!...For anyone NOT lucky enough to make it up the Palace, they're appearing on the MIDSUMMER NIGHTS TUBE SPECIAL screened on August the 16th...While on the subject of the UT's, both the single and the album, "Wild Child" (78 in the chart) are now available on picci disc, and judging by the prices being fetched for the original green picture disc for Free Yourself, you'd be well advised to stock up now.

MORE NIGHT OUT'S PLANNED Following the report that East London Mod Band, THE SCENE were headlining a COUNTDOWN NIGHT OUT (as reported in the last issue of the NEWS), we are pleased to announce that following negotiations with Ron and Nanda from the 100 CLUB in Oxford Street, we are now going to be holding these auspicious events on a "Once A Month Basis"...The second one planned is rapidly approaching (Thursday the 8th of August) and features THE SCENE, who are releasing their new "Good Lovin'" single on the same day, ably supported by THE KICK and Clacton's very own ASSISTANTS making a very long overdue London debut!! COUNTDOWN NIGHT NUMBER THREE is booked in for Thursday September 5th and will feature MAKIN' TIME as the headliners, with the support bands yet to be confirmed...It is our aim to feature three bands on every occasion in order to give value for money, and to give our promising young bands a decent venue to play, watch this space for further details...

FIVE A SIDE SOCCER COMPETITION Following the Mod Cricket league set up by a few of the more sporting ESSEX mods, it was only a matter of time until the subject of Football was raised...Quite a few people have been toying with the idea of organising something, so we here at COUNTDOWN have come up with the FIVE-A-SIDE knock out competition,something like tho one organised by "EMPTY DREAMS" between all the mod bands and fanzines back in 1980 (Extraordinary Sensations were knocked out by The Chords in the second round!!) anyway, we'd be interested in hearing from and teams (preferably of FIVE) who'd like to compete. The entry fee will be £2.50 per team, and all the money will go to providing a first and second prize to the finalists...We'd hold the competition on a knock out basis at a park in Central London, one sunday, probably in September...Any teams interested in entering, just drop us a line at our North London office.

CLUB HAPPENINGS This week we're pleased to announce two new stylist clubs in Central London...The first is on friday evenings and is called THE NUMBER ONE, admission is £1.30 (well cheap!) in Covent Garden, the second is called THE 61" and is at that Tony Class haunt, THE ROYAL OAK (Tooley Street). It's open till 2am and is a minutes walk down from the BEN TRUEMAN...See the club reviews on the inside pages for more info...

BRITISH TOP TEN: Just to please all those Merseabeat Mods in Liverpool, we've decided to feature a British TOP TEN in occasional ishs of 'news',so if you've got any fave UK Soul sounds, then just let us know and we'll sort it out, knowworrimean, john?

COUNTDOWN NEWS SHEET, 34/38 PROVOST ST, LONDON. N.1.
We are now looking for people around the country who would like to review gigs, runs and interesting mod type happenings all over the country. If you would like to contribute, just write whatever you want and send it in to our address. Now we're going weekly, we need a lot more things to write about, so get grafting.

The Phoenix
London

UPDATED WEEKLY
No. 12

★ PICKS OF
THE WEEK

A MOD SOCIETY

SIXTIES RHYTHM & SOUL CLUBS IN THE LONDON AREA

As of 5 September 1983

MONDAYS

★ + SOUND AND RHYTHM at the REGENCY SUITE, Chadwell Heath High Road (200 yds from old Greyhound). Open 8.00 - 12.00. Admission: £1.00 (£1.50 if band playing). SMART DRESS ONLY. 60's & revival Mod music.
MIDDLETON ARMS, 303 Queensbridge Rd, Dalston E8. Open 7.30-11. 60's & Mod revival music. FREE.
CHARING COUNTRY CLUB, nr. Ashford, KENT. Open 8-12. £1.00

TUESDAYS

★ + THE BUSH, Shepherds Bush. Open 8-11. £1.00. 60's & Mod revival music. (DJ: Tony Class)
+ THE CASTLE, nr. Tooting Broadway tube. Open 7-12. £1.00. 60's & Mod revival music. (DJ: Steve Kralle).

WEDNESDAYS

★ + THE ROYAL OAK, Tooley Street (London Bridge tube). Open 8-12. £1.00. 60's & Mod revival music. (DJ: Tony Class). SMART DRESS CLUB.
THE CAMDEN PALACE, Camden Town. Open 9 - 3 am. 60's & Northern Soul.
FLIPPERS at THE DOLPHIN (next to Bentals), Kingston. Open 8-10.30. £1.00 60's R & B and Northern Soul.

THURSDAYS

READY STEADY GO at BURTON'S SCHOOL OF DANCING, High Street, Old Hemel Hempstead (via A41). Open 8.30-11. £1.50. 60's & Northern Soul.
★ KING CHARLES, nr. Chatham Dockyard, Brompton, KENT. Open 7-11. £1.50 60's, Mod revival & Northern soul.

FRIDAYS

★ + THE CASTLE, nr. Tooting Broadway tube. Open 7-12. £1.00. 60's & Mod revival music. (DJ: Steve Kralle).
+ SOUND AND RHYTHM at the REGENCY SUITE, Chadwell Heath High Road (220 yards from old Greyhound). Open 8-1 am. £1.80. 60's & Mod revival music (DJs: Ray "Patriotic" & Eddie Piller). SMART DRESS ONLY.

SATURDAYS

★ + THE BUSH, SHEPHERDS BUSH HOTEL, Shepherds Bush. Open 8-11. £1.50. 60's and Mod revival music (DJ: Tony Class).
THE COCK, High Street, East Ham (5 min. from East Ham tube). Open 7-11.30. £1.00. 60's & Northern Soul.

PLEASE TURN OVER

Countdown News – Maxine Conroy, London 1985.
The Phoenix Society – Mark Johnson, London 1983.
Wot's 'Apnin' Per Mods – Tony Class, London, 1981.

159

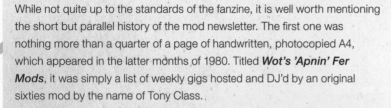

While not quite up to the standards of the fanzine, it is well worth mentioning the short but parallel history of the mod newsletter. The first one was nothing more than a quarter of a page of handwritten, photocopied A4, which appeared in the latter months of 1980. Titled **Wot's 'Apnin' Fer Mods**, it was simply a list of weekly gigs hosted and DJ'd by an original sixties mod by the name of Tony Class.

Tony, who was universally known as 'Classy', was a South London DJ and promoter who, along with Andy Ruw, was one of the first to hit upon the idea of a disco, or club night, just for mods. Up to that point, mod nights had exclusively featured bands, with an occasional record played by the likes of Jerry Floyd (an original sixties mod who was the MC at London's Marquee Club) in between sets. Tony, who often DJ'd with his brother Rob, set up a network of pubs, mainly south of the river, which catered for the same kids who went along to the Bridge House or the Wellington, just without a band.

"Imagine my frustration when I finally made it to the legal age to ride a scooter in 1967, only to see the mod scene evaporate in front of my eyes," Class told Garry Bushell in Garry's book **Time For Action**.*

"My brother Robin had bought himself a Lambretta Li 150 in 1978 and had started hanging round with Huggy Leaver and The Teenbeats down in Hastings… It brought the memories flooding back and I became determined to start up a mod disco. I finally got the chance at the tail end of '79 when me and Rob started a night at the Hercules Tavern. We soon followed in January 1980 with the Red Lion in Westminster and possibly the most famous of them all, the Walmer Castle in Peckham, a month later.

"I was amazed about how successful we were; I was 28 when I first started at the Hercules but eventually I ran 63 mod clubs and DJ'd at over 150 mod rallies or weekenders on the coast. I decided that I was going to try and keep the mod scene going for as long as I could…"

Wot's 'Apnin' Fer Mods soon took on a life of its own. Class dominated the mod scene in the early eighties and eventually attracted the attention of an American political fixer, who had washed up in London looking for something to do… and he chose mod.

Mark Johnson worked for Ronald Reagan's political team but he had been bitten by the mod bug on a visit to the UK and decided to relocate to these shores, buy a scooter and join in on the fun. Within a matter of months he had put his not-inconsiderable organisational skills into setting up a quasi-masonic 'mod society', which he called the Phoenix Society.

Johnson rode a white Vespa adorned with the legend 'Behold the pale horse' (although I was certain that biblical references about the four horsemen of the apocalypse sailed over the heads of most teenage mods), and soon earned the nickname 'The General'. In his mid-thirties,

Time For Action: The Mod Revival 1978–1981 was published in 2012 by Countdown Books and is a history of the scene and its influence from the first music journalist to cover the scene in the mainstream press.

The Phoenix Society — Mark Johnson
London 1983.
Wot's 'Apnin' Fer Mods — Tony Class
London, 1981.

WEEK-BEGINNING 25 JANUARY 1984   No. 33

THE PHOENIX LIST

SIXTIES DISCOS AND EVENTS IN THE LONDON AREA

PUBLISHED EVERY WEDNESDAY by THE PHOENIX-LONDON (A Mod Society) and distributed free at THE ROYAL OAK (Wed.), LORDS (Thurs.), ROCKAFELLA CENTER in Carnaby St. (Sat.), SNEAKERS at THE BUSH (Sun.), and THE DOLPHIN in KINGSTON (Wed.).
-- Additions or corrections? Phone MARK JOHNSON on 402 0123 (days) --

THE 1984 SOUTHERN MOD AND NATIONAL SCOOTER RUNS

14-15 APR -- CLACTON (MOD)	14-15 JUL -- BOURNEMOUTH (MOD)/
20-23 APR -- MORECAMBE (NAT'L)	DUNBAR, SCOTLAND (NAT'L)
28-29 APR -- MARGATE (MOD)	4-5 AUG ----- TENBY, S WALES (NAT'L)
5-7 MAY ---- TORQUAY (NAT'L)	18-19 AUG -- HASTINGS (MOD)
26-28 MAY -- GREAT YARMOUTH (NAT'L)	25-27 AUG -- ISLE OF WIGHT (NAT'L)
23-24 JUN -- BRIGHTON (MOD)	15-16 SEP -- SKEGNESS (NAT'L)
	6-7 OCT ----- WESTON-SUPER-MARE(NAT'L)

WEDNESDAY, 25 JANUARY 1984

▶ THE TRUTH live at SAVOY BALLROOM, THE BOSTON ARMS, Tufnell Park. £3.50
      Support: THE PLAYN JAYN and THE STINGRAYS.
+ THE ROYAL OAK, Tooley Street (London Bridge tube). Open 8-12. £1.00
   60's & Mod revival music. (DJ: Tony Class). SMART DRESS CLUB.
   PROOF OF AGE REQUIRED.
+ THE DUKE OF CLARENCE, Frampton Street (off Edgware Rd) NW.8. 8-11. £1.00
   THE CAMDEN PALACE, Camden Town. Open 9 - 3 am. 60's Dance Pop, R & B, and
   Soul £3.00
   FLIPPERS at THE DOLPHIN (next to Bentals), Kingston. Open 8-10.30. £1.00
   60's R & B (DJ: PAUL HALLAM) and Northern Soul (DJ: Tony Sheene).

THURSDAY, 26 JANUARY 1984

   THE SCENE, LONG TALL SHORTY, DIRECT HITS live at the 100 CLUB, 100 Oxford
      Street, W.1.
▶ + SOUND AND RHYTHM at LORDS (100 yards from ILFORD Britrail). Open 8 - late.
   £1.50 (before 9.30) then £1.80. Sixties & Mod revival music.
   (DJ's: Ray "Patriotic" & Eddie Piller). SMART DRESS ONLY!
   READY STEADY GO at BURTON'S SCHOOL OF DANCING, High Street, Old Hemel
      Hempstead (via A41). Open 8.30-11. £1.50. 60's & N. soul
   KING CHARLES, nr. Chatham Dockyard, Brompton, KENT. Open 7-11. £1.50
      60's, Mod revival & Northern soul.

FRIDAY, 27 JANUARY 1984

   THE PLOUGH, Kingsbury Road (opposite Express Dairy), NW.9. Open 8-11.
      FREE! 60's and Northern soul.

THE PHOENIX LIST often promotes events which THE PHOENIX-LONDON feels encourages the Mod movement: small bands, good clubs, Mod scooter runs, etc. But we do not do advertising. If there are any rubber stamps on this list, please boycott those rip-off merchants or products.

JUNE 11th 1981   WHAT'S 'APNIN' FER MODS   ISSUE TWENTY FOUR

SATURDAYS   'THE BUSH HOTEL' CORNER OF SHEPHERDS BUSH GREEN + GOLDHAWK ROAD. ENTRANCE IN GOLDHAWK ROAD. PARKING IN ALLEY BETWEEN PUB AND B.B.C. THEATRE. NEAREST TUBE SHEPHERDS BUSH.
SUNDAYS   TO BE ARRANGED.
MONDAYS   'THE PHOENIX' CAVENDISH SQUARE W.1.
TUESDAYS   'NIGHTMOVES' REAR OF THE CASTLE, TOOTING HIGH STREET S.W.17. OPEN 8-12. PRIVATE CAR PARK AVAILABLE (FREE) NEAREST TUBE TOOTING BROADWAY.
THURSDAYS   CARD HOLDERS ONLY. (PROOF OF AGE REQUIRED)
FRIDAYS   'THE HOPE' JUNCTION OF COWCROSS ST. + (LOWER) ST. JOHN ST. E.C.1. PARKING IN FRONT OF PUB. NEAREST TUBE FARRINGDON ST.

COMING EVENT

FRIDAY 19th JUNE (NEXT FRIDAY) 8.00 P.M. TILL 1.00 A.M. RIVERDALE HALL LOUNGE SUITE, (INSIDE SHOPPING PRECINCT) LEWISHAM HIGH ST. S.E.13. PARKING IN CUL-DE-SAC BY THE SIDE OF THE HALL IN RENNELL ST. TICKETS ON SALE FROM ME ONLY. MEMBERS £1.50 NON-MEMBERS £2.00. THERE HAS BEEN A BAND BOOKED FOR THIS EVENT WHICH I HAVE SEEN PERSONALLY AT RONNIE SCOTTS, BY THE NAME OF EYE AND THE QUATERBOYS AND THEY HAVE A GREAT TAMLA MOTOWN SOUND
                                          TONY CLASS DJ.

JUNE 25th 1981   WITS 'APNIN' FR MODS   ISSUE TWENTY-FIVE.

MONDAYS   'THE ROYAL FORT' GRANGE RD. OFF TOWER BRIDGE RD. S.E. THIS TIME WE HAVE THE ENTIRE PUB. ONLY MODS WILL BE ALLOWED IN. BUSES 1 & 78 FROM THE ELEPHANT & CASTLE.
TUESDAYS   'NIGHTMOVES' REAR OF THE CASTLE. TOOTING HIGH ST. S.W.17. OPEN 8-12 PRIVATE CAR PARK AVAILABLE (FREE) NEAREST TUBE TOOTING BROADWAY.
THURSDAYS   CARD HOLDERS ONLY (PROOF OF AGE REQUIRED)
FRIDAYS   'THE HOPE' JUNCTION OF COWCROSS ST. AND (LOWER) ST. JOHN ST E.C.1. PARKING IN FRONT OF PUB. NEAREST TUBE FARRINGDON ST
SATURDAYS   JULY 11th 'THE BUSH HOTEL'.
SUNDAY   'AUTOPUB' 'CHEQUERED FLAG' EAST LANE NORTH WEMBLEY OPPOSITE NORTH WEMBLEY STATION (BAKERLOO LINE) CAR PARK AVAILABLE AT SIDE OF PUB.
                                          TONY CLASS D.J.

JULY 2nd 1981   WOTS 'APNIN' FER MODS   ISSUE TWENTY SIX

SATURDAY   4th JULY FOR ONE NIGHT ONLY 'PHOENIX' OXFORD CIRCUS W.1.
SATURDAYS   AS FROM 11th JULY 'THE BUSH HOTEL' SHEPHERDS BUSH. ENTRANCE IN GOLD-HAWK RD NEAREST TUBE SHEPHERDS BUSH.
SUNDAYS   TO BE ARRANGED (CHEQUERED FLAG) NO LONGER OK.
MONDAYS   'THE ROYAL FORT' GRANGE RD S.E.1.(OFF TOWER BRIDGE RD) PARKING IN FRONT OF PUB. BUSES 1 & 78.
TUESDAYS   'NIGHTMOVES' REAR OF 'THE CASTLE' TOOTING HIGH ST. SW17 NEAREST STN. TOOTING BROADWAY. OPEN 8-12 CAR PARK AVAILABLE FREE.
THURSDAYS   CARD-HOLDERS ONLY. (PROOF OF AGE REQUIRED).
FRIDAYS   'THE HOPE' JUNCTION OF COWCROSS ST. & (LOWER) ST. JOHN ST. E.C.1. PARKING IN FRONT OF PUB. NEAREST TUBE FARRINGDON ST.

COMING EVENT

THERE IS AN ORGANISED RUN TO BRIGHTON ON AUGUST 8th A VENUE IS BEING ARRANGED AND ALSO WE ARE TRYING TO GET PERMISSION TO PLAY RECORDS ON THE BEACH.
                                          TONY CLASS D.J.

he was a good 15 years older than most others on the scene. However, his organisational skills were second to none. The Phoenix Society began as half a dozen promoters and DJs (including Tony Class and Paul Hallam) who would meet in dingy pub function rooms, and it soon grew into the biggest and best pre-internet mod information service. As well as running the society, Johnson edited *The Phoenix List*, a weekly newsletter that featured news stories and, most importantly, gig and club listings pertinent to the scene.

Paul Hallam recalls: "I picked up a copy of *The Phoenix List* and read about a club called the Regency Suite over in East London. Up to this point, most of the clubs we knew about were Classy's, either through West London word of mouth or the *Wot's 'Apnin' Fer Mods* newsletter. So I trekked over to Chadwell Heath to hear Eddie Piller play in the spring of '83 and met Pete Holland, who proposed me for the Phoenix Society. The main thing I remember was that we met in a rundown old pub called the Griffin in Shoreditch, full of redundant, old East End printers and out-of-work whores! I was accepted into the society and embraced my membership, but the Phoenix took a lot of stick for trying to turn the mod scene into a regimented thing, rather like the Boy Scouts. But on the other hand, Johnson did the scene a lot of good, well… *The Phoenix List* certainly helped perpetuate my DJ career!"

The Phoenix List soon became an indispensable part of the vibrant and growing mid-eighties London mod scene but, more importantly, it provided a template for many to follow.

Maxine Conroy, one of the directors of Countdown Records, which by 1985 had assumed the position of 'home' to the latest generation of mod bands, remembers the part her own newsletter, *Countdown News*, played.

"Eddie Piller and Terry Rawlings had come to Countdown from *Extraordinary Sensations* and consequently were full of the added value a regular mailing list and information service could bring to the label. We looked at how Mark Johnson produced *The Phoenix List* and simply copied it. He had a very successful format, which was four A4 pages reduced to an A5 size – very simple to make, as in '85, even basic photocopiers had a reduction facility. Once reduced, the whole newsletter could be printed or copied onto a simple A4 double-sided sheet, folded in half and slipped into an envelope. I think at Countdown Records, peak we had around 6,000 subscribers who received their copy of *Countdown News* in exchange for a second-class stamp every other week. A solid and successful marketing system before the internet was even invented."

Newsletters flourished throughout the 1980s. They also tended to be published more regularly. Fanzines could often take months to prepare, with interviews and detailed graphic content. By their very nature, newsletters were short, concise, informative.

The Phoenix Society – Mark Johnson
London 1983/1984.
Countdown News – Maxine Conroy
London 1985/1987.

PART WEEK BEGINNING 17 FEBRUARY 1984 NO. 36

THE PHOENIX LIST

PUBLISHED EVERY WEDNESDAY (except this week due to the vote on the Clacton Run) for THE PHOENIX-LONDON (A Mod Society) and distributed free at THE ROYAL OAK (Wed.), LORDS (Thurs.), "SNEAKERS" at THE BUSH (Sun.), and THE DOLPHIN in KINGSTON (Wed.), and by request at ROCKAFELLA CENTER and RIGHT TRACK RECORDS IN Carnaby Street (Sat.). Edited by MARK JOHNSON and all comments, additions, and/or corrections to him at 27 Sale Place, London W2 1PT. (01-402 7360)

CLACTON at EASTER!

The result of 500 ballots distributed last week came out in favour of holding the Clacton Southern Mods Scooter run on Easter Bank Holiday. Now that that has been sorted out, we'd like to say that the National Runs are as well -- but no such luck. The new Scootermania (No.26) declined to give the run dates, so we will have to wait until we hear from the elusive and ailing Martin Dixon. Below are those runs which have finalised, confirmed, and set dates:

THE 1984 SOUTHERN MOD AND NATIONAL SCOOTER RUNS

21-23 APR --- CLACTON (MOD)
21-23 APR --- MORECAMBE (NAT'L)
28-29 APR --- MARGATE (MOD)
5-7 MAY ----- TORQUAY (NAT'L)
26-28 MAY --- GREAT YARMOUTH (NAT'L)
23-24 JUN -- BRIGHTON (MOD)
14-15 JUL -- BOURNEMOUTH (MOD)
14-15 JUL -- DUNBAR, SCOTLAND (NAT'L)
4-5 AUG ---- TENBY, S. WALES (NAT'L)
18-19 AUG -- HASTINGS (MOD)
25-27 AUG -- ISLE OF WIGHT (NAT'L)

STEVE MARRIOTT & THE PACKET OF THREE GIG IN LONDON

Steve Marriott (once lead singer of THE MOMENTS, SMALL FACES, HUMBLE PIE, SMALL FACES II, BLIND DRUNK (of Bridgehouse fame) and HUMBLE PIE II) is back in London for six weeks. With Jimmy Leverton (former FAT MATRESS bassist) and Dave Hines (former SPENCER DAVIS drummer) he is rehearsing as PACKET OF THREE (we'll leave that to your imagination). With upcoming (but yet-to-be-confirmed) dates pencilled in for The Venue (with FAST EDDIE in support?!?), Camden Dingwalls and Woolwich Tram Shed, PACKET OF THREE play their debut gig at Benny's in Old Harlow this Friday, 17 February.

NATIONAL MOD MEETING

After the Southern Mod Runs are completed (and to celebrate 1984 -- the year of twenty years of Mod scooter runs), there will be a national All-Mod Con(vention) held in London. Taking place in November, it will be open to all Mods and all Mods attending have an equal vote and an equal say -- this is what the word democracy is all about. The Southern Mod Scooter Runs (which are runs in the South, not runs set up for/by Southern Mods) will be chosen for 1985, and as many people as possible will have a turn at the microphone to give their ideas and opinions. Ronnie Lane, bassist for Small Faces, has volunteered to give the opening speech. After the meeting there will be a disco (£2 entry) which will feature the hottest Mod band of the moment. Comments? Suggestions? The address to write to is above.

COUNTDOWN

34–38 PROVOST ST, LONDON N1 7QY | TELEPHONE: 01-250 0398

ISSUE SEVENTEEN

There's no silly introduction line in this issue, we were bored with "Hi there and other equally mundane and boring lies, so it's straight into the info... Dear readers...how have you been since last week?...Oh, sorry, I thought we weren't doing that this week...OK, let's get on with it for God's sake... Can't you tell that it's not been a busy week ? Yeah ? Oh...sorry...

Well CHRISTMAS is soon to be upon us once again, and nothing is stirring in the office, not even a mouse etc...So in order for you all to join in with our 'good will to all etc...' we've organised a COUNTDOWN CHRISTMAS NITE OUT, no, don't stop reading already...This one's really special, it's at the Clarendon Hotel Ballroom (that's the upstairs bit) on Friday the 13th (see, even the date's special) and topping the bill, in a double Headliner are both MAKIN' TIME AND THE PRISONERS, who will be ably assisted by THE KICK and the first ever appearance and performance of former chief-Chord Billy Hassett and his band since leaving these fair shores for Ireland back in those dark days of '81...We've even laid on a comedian to keep you all amused...Isn't that really special?

The tickets are at the Yule-time price of £3.00 in advance from the Countdown Office (if writing in please include an SAE) or £4 on the night...The doors open at 7.45 and continue through till 12.00 midnight...You will have noticed that we've moved venues for this, cos Ebenezer down the hundred club was heard to condemn the whole excercise as 'Humbug'.!!

Half of our Christmas Bill MAKIN' TIME and THE KICK are warming up a week proir to this with a gig at the Birmingham BARREL ORGAN in Birmingham on the 2nd of December, while the Prisoners step out this week with another date at the hundred club (see the advert at the bottom of the page for further info.)

The UNTOUCHABLES gig at this years GLASTONBURY FESTIVAL was recorded by the BBC for 'broadcasting at a later date', well finally, that'later date' seems to have arrived and it's to be aired on Saturday the 23rd of November at 6.30 on their 'IN CONCERT' programme...Turn On, Tune In, Drop Out...(Eh ??)

Anyone who saw the TUBE last week will be as mystified as us as to the appearance of a strange man in a Prisoners T Shirt proclaiming that the band would be appeaing on a programme later on in the series...As niether us (their record label) or they (the band) know nothing about it, we can only suppose that The TUBE means to repeat the issue from the first series where our caped crusaders appeared strumming away in STAR TREK uniforms...boldy going where no band had gone before...We'll chase up the programmes producers and fill you in next issue...

Don't forget that subscriptions are still available to anyone who would like to recieve this wonderfull publication (rubbish for short) through their door (first class post, of course) every week, just send us in two pounds and we'll send you the next ten consecutive issues of THE NEWS...As usual, single issues are available for an SAE...A new mail-order record list will be available from us as from next week...Must stop typing now, before I type over the advert...

THE PRISONERS
COUNTDOWN NITE
21st NOV
100
THE DAGGERMEN
THE BOTTOM LINE

COUNTDOWN

34–38 PROVOST ST, LONDON N1 7QY | TELEPHONE: 01-250 0398

Issue SIXTEEN is here on time, and this one is going to have an extra large distribution of 3,000...Yep, we're producing the extra large number to cater for the National Mod Meeting that is being held in PETERBOROUGH this saturday and also for the mail out to everyone on the mailing list in order to advertise the release of the new Makin' Time sinlge "FEELS LIKE IT'S LOVE" which was released last wednesday, and went in the top 200 at number 124 after only three days sales...Those of you who've seen COUNTDOWN NEWS before may remember that the bands last single "HERE IS MY NUMBER" stayed in the top 200 for fourteen weeks but didn't manage to break into the top hundred...Still we're hoping for better things from this one...One single that did manage to get into the hundred was SPECTRUM'S "ALL OR NOTHING" (the Mod Aid single for Ethiopia and Multiple Sclirosis)which, after a dissapinting start (due to disqualification by GALLUP for the first week for 'suspected chart interference' went in at number 93 and has remained reasonably steady this week at number 96...Also,hanging on in the indie-charts is THE GENTS whose "STAY WITH ME" is at number 44...Expect a chart update Next Issue...

Anybody wanting to recieve COUNTDOWN NEWS on a regular basis just has to send £2.00 sterling (£3.00 for U.S. or £2.50 for Europe) to cover the cost of first class (or Airmail) post...Anyone just wanting to reciever the odd issue should just send us an SAE and we'll forward you the current issue...

A mail order record service is also available...List on request...

The SILENCE one of the only two British SKA/ROCKSTEADY bands I know that are in existance (the other being the brilliant POTATO FIVE) have set up an information service...You can contact them at FLAT 4, Nyali Lodge,9 Heatherley Rd. Camberley, Surrey for details of forthcoming gigs and events.

Mark Johnson informes me that the forthcoming MOD-AID alldayer that's scheduled at The Walthamstow Assembly Hall on the 15th of December has sold over two hundred tickets in four days, and there are only eight hundred left...The full list of bands appearing was printed in last weeks News, and the tickets cost £10 (of which every penny goes to Charity) and are available from THE PHOENIX LIST, MERC or CARNABY CAVERN...

THE UNTOUCHABLES who are currently touring round Europe, release their new 45 next week... "What's Gone Wrong" is the third single to be released in the UK by the band, and represents much more of a REGGAE sound than both their previous efforts...It's a totally new version of the song and it's sung by one of the new band members...As soon as they get back from Europe, The UT's are back off on the second part of their UK tour with MAKIN'TIME, here are the dates that are presently available; Tue 19th NOV: Brighton Coasters. Wed 20th Egham Royal College. Thur 21st Leicester University. Fri 22nd Oxford Polytechnic. Sat 23rd. Coventry Polytechnic. Sun 24th Norwich U.E.A. Tues 26th Preston Poly Wed 27th Stafford College. Thur 28th Newcastle University and Saturday the 30t November at Manchester University. The only London date on the tour is also with MAKIN' TIME and is at the CAMDEN PALACE, Sunday the 1st of DECEMBER....

The KICK
&
THE BOTTOM LINE
13th NOV.
THE CRICKETERS
at the oval.

COUNTDOWN

COUNTDOWN NEWS SHEET - ISSUE NUMBER]2 - WEDNESDAY 2nd OCTOBER - PUBLISHED WEEKLY

Countdown News is published within the first three days of each week, and is available by sending a SAE to our office at 34#38 Provost Street, London N.1. Alternatively, you may prefer to recieve the News Sheet through your door every week. This costs 2 Pounds for a ten week period. (2.50 for Europe)...We also have a mail order record list that is updated every two weeks, available on request.

The most dissapointing piece of news to reach us this week, is the last minute postponement of the 'Pirate' run to Southend that had been scheduled for this coming weekend...The exact details of why the "CRAWDADDY WEEKEND AWAY" has had to be cancelled are so far a bit hazy...It seems that someone at the club that Southend DJ Chad had booked, has done the proverbial runner with the deposit payed out for the venue, and consequently the club's manager has called a halt to the proceedings-This came as a major dissapointment to Chad, who had been working very hard towards a successfull run to Southend, after Mark Johnson and Tony Class decided to ban the venue for being too 'provocative' earlier this year. Anybody who has purchased an advance ticket is assured of getting a refund...Further details of this upset will be published next week, when we've had a chance to talk to some of the parties concerned...No alternative has been arranged, because everything happened at such short notice, so if you're planning to venture out this weekend, all that's on is: Friday, The Oasis Club, Old Kent Rd, (Soul till 2.00 and only One pound fifty to get in).Saturday, The Ben Truman in Southwark St, followed by The Royal Oak in Tooley St (doors open till 2.00)...Sundays is still Sneakers at The Bush (doors shut at]0.30...)

Mark Johnson has just announced that he intends to take his Mod Aid project one step further. Following the release of the Mod Aid single "All Or Nothing" next week he has announced plans to hold a Mod Live Aid concert at The Walthamstow Town Hall on the First of December...The doors will be open at]].00 for twelve hours, and the bar will be open at normal drinking times. There is a limited capacity of 1000, and tickets will cost Ten Pounds. Needless to say,all the money raised will be donated to the two charities that benefited from the single...Bands so far in the line up are: (in alphabetical order) The CO STARS. The CREATION,The DANSETTE The DIRECT HITS,ELEANOR RIGBY, The GENTS, The JETSET, The MOMENT, The RAGE, The RISK, The SCENE SOLID STATE, The THREADS, The TIMES, The Tommy JAMES QUARTET, The WAY OUT, XL and YEA YEA... A few other groups are expected to be added to the line up. Tickets will be available from The Phoenix List in due course. It is a Smart Dress Only event, and anybody wearing anything apart from trousers won't be admitted...

Contary to what was said a couple of issues ago in The NEWS about The MOMENT not having their single released by DIAMOND and moving over to RAVE records, well, one of the lads in Rough Trade's distribution centre rung me up this morning to let me have the months new releases, and lo and behold, One of them was "],2, They Fly" by Haverhill's finest...I can't imagine what's gone on there, but I do know that the single, (recorded almost a year ago) is now available. OK ,..

The twelve inch mix of the new Makin' Time single will certainly shock a few of our more conservative type of listeners, keep yer ears peeled...

Makin Time
THE B-TEAM
THE WAY OUT
COUNTDOWN NITE OUT
at 100
15 oct

Issue SIXTEEN is here on time, and this one is going to have an extra large
distribution of 3,000...Yeo, we're producing the extra large number to cater
for the National Mod Meeting that is being held in PETERBOROUGH this saturd-

Bernadine Wood remembers: "I think everyone was aware of **The Phoenix List.** It was okay for gig listings but I much preferred the fanzines where people had gone to a lot of trouble to interview bands or had done articles about a rally or an event. They made more interesting reading and connected you with like-minded people. Newsletters were just information sheets really."

While newsletters had virtually disappeared by the mid-nineties, new fanzine titles were still making it into print.

One of the most forward-thinking and progressive editors active towards the end of the pre-internet print days was Gordon Wallace, who was based in Birmingham in the mid-to late nineties His first project, **Hey Sa Lo Ney** (the rather odd title being inspired by the Micky Lee Lane/Action mod soul classic) morphed into the highly rated **Moke** fanzine. But it was his next project, **Lumumba**, that is virtually unique in the world of mod fanzines, as it was one of the very few examples of a truly original, fully illustrated comic. Here he tells his story.

"I previously wrote fanzines in the eighties, based around promoting local indie bands and poetry – it was all influenced by Paul Weller's Riot Stories publishing imprint, followed closely by **Jamming!**, the fanzine, and later bona fide magazine, edited by Tony Fletcher. The northern end of the mod revival movement in the eighties provided an underground to try out lots of ideas, and I got in touch with a lot of good people – an early eighties Prestwick-based modzine called **Stepping Stone** was a particular favourite, as it mixed left-wing politics with mod revival music.

"**Moke** modzine came out of a short-lived A5 black and white idea called **Hey Sah Lo Ney**, aiming eventually to be a mod/jazz-influenced version of Paul Bradshaw's jazz magazine **Straight No Chaser**, with the emphasis on Blue Note design and Vespa attitude. Visually I was aiming for the **Straight No Chaser** design (which I loved!) and editorially it was all about pushing the parameters of the genre. Sometimes I'd be interviewing Spanish mod revival bands talking about the emerging political climate there, and then I'd be speaking to Japanese bands, like UFO, about batucada*. With desktop publishing becoming more mainstream, I tried to push the boundaries of presentation, which meant colour inserts and larger formats – and I also had access to a quarter-million pound printer thanks to my job at the time, which allowed me to do more complicated and bigger print runs. I was interested in pushing the literary side of things, too. It received good reviews in **Record Collector**.

"I read a lot of independent comics and wanted to do something scooter/mod-based, which is where **Lumumba** came from. Producing a completely hand-drawn comic on your own is a lot of hard work, though. A few panels started out in Helen Barrell's **Dansette** and then I produced a single issue, working on it every night for a month."

The Phoenix Society – Mark Johnson, London 1988.
Countdown News – Maxine Conroy, London 1985.
Moke – Gordon Wallace, Birmingham 1999.

*Batucada is a type of Brazilian, African-influenced fast-paced samba music.

Moke—
Gordon
Wallace,
Birmingham
1999.

As previously mentioned, *Lumumba* is one of the only hand-drawn comics on the mod scene. Artist and fanzine editor Terry Rawlings explains why: "Technology has moved on so much in the last 20 years but in the nineties every single cell or frame would have needed to be hand-drawn (in the same way that the A5 *Commando* comics were) that I would take such a long time that it just wouldn't have been possible. Now things are different, though."

The only publication of a similar ilk was not actually a fanzine but a hardback book by the legendary British comic illustrator Dave Gibbons. *The Originals*, published in 2004, pitted the mods against the rockers in a futuristic war.

Outside of zines and newsletters, a number of specialist magazines emerged, but they had production values more akin to the glossies.

Shindig!, edited by John Mojo Mills, was very much produced in the spirit of fanzines, despite it being a professional magazine. One of Paul Weller's favourite things, the magazine sits alongside *Record Collector* in the racks at WH Smith. Both magazines incorporated regular features and articles that mods could appreciate.

Ian McCann, for many years *Record Collector*'s editor, understood the value of the specialist world. "People who spend their life interested in a specialist scene invest a lot of themselves in it. They really care about music."

Scootering, too, has long been a champion of the mod scene and has enjoyed an enormous level of sales via high street newsagents. While numerous pages are dedicated to the music scene, by its very nature *Scootering* is most definitely a publication for those who ride Vespas and Lambrettas, with a bit of 'mod culture' bolted on.

However, with the dawning of the internet age, fanzines became virtually obsolete, to be replaced by blogs and websites, and in order to find the contemporary versions of the mod fanzine, one must go online.

Paul Weller agrees. "The modern take on a fanzine is definitely the blog or the dedicated website. I really like [the men's fashion site] *His Knibs* and *modculture.co.uk*, as I think they tie in with my personal view of mod."

The internet provided numerous opportunities for archive sites, which to a large degree have fulfilled the 'historical information and education' obligation Chords drummer Buddy Ascott thought was so important to the role of the 1979 originating editors. One such, self-dubbed 'The Online Mod/ern/ist Archive', is the blog *Jack That Cat Was Clean*, which is named after the legendary R&B track from Dr. Horse and was established by the Belgian pair Jean-Marc Vos and the late Thierry Steuve. Without much

Lumumba — Gordon Wallace, Birmingham 1996.

contemporary comment, the site is a collection of articles gleaned from any source discussing or reflecting on the original mods.*

Fredrik Ekander, one of the founders of the Swedish mod website *Uppers*, explains why he set up the site at the dawn of the internet age.

"You could see the potential of the internet to expand and improve on the concept of a fanzine. We set up *Uppers* as a club in 1987 and the website as soon as it became practical to do so, which was around 1997.

"With a fanzine you are limited in terms of space, you find yourself restricted to what you can accommodate; with the internet, the content is literally limitless. At its peak Uppers had more than 50 regular contributors and an archive of more than 700 articles, all available at the click of a link. We pioneered the concept of a 'city guide', by which I mean that we asked mods to compile a list of record and clothes shops, bars, clubs and even cinemas that might have been considered mod friendly in their particular city and we then expanded that by adding details for club nights or gigs. It really worked, too. I remember about 15 years ago, my job had taken me to Madrid, Spain, for a couple of days and I found myself at a loose end on a Saturday night. I clicked on to *Uppers* and discovered that Eddie Piller was playing a DJ gig alongside Eneida Fever less than two miles from my hotel."

Fredrik's site enjoyed much success over a long period of time, but like so many who run a fanzine, it is ultimately a labour of love and the need to engage with real life often gets in the way.

Fredrik again: "Even though there were a number of us involved, in the end it was just too much to keep the site going – we didn't make a conscious effort to stop, in the end it just kind of faded away. It was of its time and was a brilliant thing to have been involved with."

David Walker of the British modernist website *Modculture* has made it work by hosting a number of specialist websites (for example, that cover film and television) and providing them with a commercial and professional edge. Paul Weller's internet destination of choice, *modculture.co.uk* is a superb website that shows just what can be achieved if you have the time and determination to create something special.

David tells us how he got into the mod scene and why he decided to set up his site. "I was an avid fanzine reader and actually wrote for some football fanzines as well as writing music reviews for various publications, which tended to be aligned to my taste at the time, which was jangly indie pop and the paisley underground. By the time I got on the mod scene proper, fanzines had grown up a bit and some were up there with magazines, although there were still the 'newsletter' formats kicking about. The pick of the bunch for me was the *New Breed* by Paul Welsby and Neil Henderson, which was a cracking read. I've been looking at republishing some of those articles on *Modculture*."

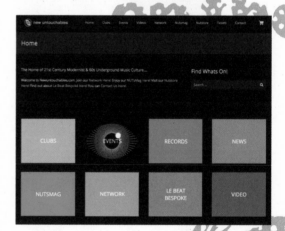

Jack That Cat was Clean – Jean-Marc Vos and the late Thierry Steuve, online blog 2007/2015.
The New Untouchables – Rob Bailey, website, ongoing.
Modculture – David Walker, website, ongoing.
His Knibs – David Walker, online blog, ongoing.
NutsMag – Rob Bailey, London 2011.

Fanzines once undertook this task. We at *Extraordinary Sensations* would often cut and paste articles about sixties mods, which we'd purloined from original sources, in our perceived role to provide unvarnished information and to educate the next generation of young mods.

"In the north, there didn't seem much of a network for mods in the late 1990s, so the northern mods mailing list was set up for like-minded people to keep in touch in the early days of the internet. *Modculture* came off the back of that; it was a reference guide for people new to mod, a mix of listings and recommended listening and reading for anyone who might be inquisitive about mod at that time. It was a social network before the term was invented, especially once the forum was added in. The features and listings would have worked in print, but the interactivity and chat obviously wouldn't."

"Saying that, I always viewed *Modculture* as an online fanzine and I still do, in fact. I don't have anything to sell or plug, so I just write about what appeals to me from a mod point of view as and when I see it. It's as much a labour of love as any printed fanzine."

David even considered publishing a collection of his work in printed form: "I did look at producing a print version a few years in, a monthly or quarterly publication with unique content away from the site. I even had a publisher do some mock-ups for it and, to be honest, it looked amazing. But the problem, which is perhaps common to people who run both websites and fanzines, is time.

"*Modculture* has always been a hobby rather than a job and it seemed impossible to oversee a print magazine/fanzine, as well as the website and a job. So I had to park the idea. Interestingly, I have never had as many people approach me to contribute to *Modculture* than when I floated the print version. For all its merits, there is always more prestige in appearing in print than online, and there always will be."

At the time, the online fanzine concept was in its infancy.

"The only other similar entity to *Modculture* when I started was *Uppers*, which was a site I loved but was probably more wide-ranging than just 'mod'. Thinking back, this was the late 1990s and mod online was really just a couple of sites (a US one called *The Boiler* was prominent and had a members-only policy, if I recall), some email lists and a couple of sites that promoted clubs and organisations, like Rob Bailey's *The New Untouchables* for example. Competition was thin on the ground.

"If I'm honest, competition isn't something that bothers me. As I said earlier, I have always viewed *Modculture* as a personal online fanzine with occasional contributors here and there. It isn't a business, it's just a hobby and an outlet for things I love."

Despite the commercial potential the internet offers, *Modculture* has struggled to break even.

"The site might well have cost me more over the years than it makes back in revenue. I've had offers to sell it in the past and in hindsight that might not have been a bad move. *Modculture* isn't cheap to run and needs a redesign every few years, which again is costly. I do get some ad revenue in and some affiliate money [a small cut of the sale of related items through the website]. I reckon it probably breaks even these days but that's about it. I could turn it into a commercial entity, sell my own range of designs, stick up more obviously commercial content, and possibly even sell off some of the site to brands. But I think that would change the site's dynamic completely. Perhaps there's some middle ground somewhere."

The Mod Generation is a more mainstream site that features an enormous number of articles alongside a forum, allowing real-time discussion with other like-minded people around the world – which, in the pre-internet days, would have been relegated to snail mail.

But the internet explosion has not meant the end of the printed word. Dublin's *Sussed* was a highly professional full-colour fanzine established by Joe Moran and Ray Gilligan that ran for half a dozen glorious issues. Likewise, Drew Hipson's *Modernist* is a full-colour magazine that often features the likes of Paul Weller or Noel Gallagher on the cover.

Adam Cooper explains what drives a contemporary mod fanzine editor to compete with websites: "I think because people like to have something to hold, something tangible to collect. Mods and those with an interest in the scene by definition are collectors, and most who kindly buy *Heavy Soul!* will probably have collections of other zines they bought in their youth. I grew up buying fanzines from Carnaby Street in the mid-eighties and the info inside was so valuable. That is kinda what I try to achieve with *Heavy Soul!* Getting interviews is the main part of the zine. In the past I've interviewed members of sixties legendary bands, like The MeddyEvils, Untamed, Nolan Porter, The Who, The Bo Street Runners, Misunderstood, The Eyes, as well as '79 heroes like The Chords, Purple Hearts, The Scooters. I mix this with pieces on artists and photographers, right up to the people who keep the scene going today. I still flick through my old zines from time to time for inspiration and nostalgia reasons; it's just something I can do and it's a thrill to put it all together. Information on the internet is quite throwaway and forgettable, but if it's in print, what you are trying to get across resonates more."

Adam originally established the fanzine to help promote his vinyl releases.

"I had a record label for a few years before the zine but rebranded into Heavy Soul Records in order to incorporate the new label and fanzine. Early issues had a vinyl release with each copy, but now they have a 25-track 'Club Soul' CD free with each issue. *Heavy Soul!* Issue 1 came out in 2010 and now, at mid-2018, I am putting together Issue 43.

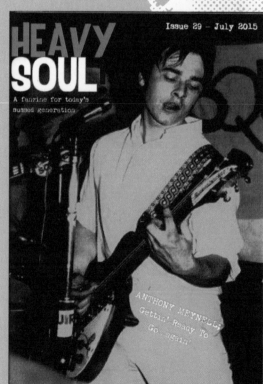

Heavy Soul! – Adam Cooper, Milton Keynes 2015.
Sussed – Joe Moran and Ray Gilligan, Dublin 1996.
Modernist – Drew Hipson, Glasgow 2016.

"Issues 1 to 3 were A4, numbers 4 up to 36 were A5, and 36 to 39 were back to A4 and still black and white, but from Issue 39 I went all-colour, with a distinct magazine style while still keeping that fanzine aura and vibe going. There are spelling mistakes, bad grammar and other basic mistakes, which keeps it real I think..."

But the glory days of fanzine sales are a distant memory. *Extraordinary Sensations* was probably the most successful modzine, hitting sales of over 15,000 at its peak, but as Terry Rawlings says: "We were running the fanzine as a full-time job. We visited the office every day and we worked really hard at it, it took over our lives for three or four years. I doubt there is either the market or the will for that ever to happen again..."

Adam Cooper agrees: "Unfortunately, it's not the 1980s any more, when fanzines sold in their thousands. I sell roughly 100-plus copies each issue, which sometimes doesn't even cover the printing cost now I've upgraded to colour, but it's a labour of love. It sometimes depends on who's on the front and inside. Earlier issues with The Strypes or Weller on the cover sold well. Mass-produced magazines like *Mojo* or *Shindig* have money behind them to push their brand, as well as teams of contributors and sales people behind them, which is great but I like to keep it simple – the people who read *Heavy Soul!* are sussed enough to know everything inside is from the heart."

And that just about sums up mod fanzines – they were, and indeed are always from the heart.

The last word goes to David Walker, creator of the online fanzine *Modculture*.

"If I see or read about a fanzine, I'm always interested. I still buy magazines too. Maybe it's part nostalgia, but it is probably down to knowing it will be the end result of a lot of work and dedication. The print media has a prestige status that the internet can't match. Anyone could set up a website in a day. But setting up a fanzine or magazine takes a lot more work and planning. Just like vinyl is still strong in the world of downloads, printed media will still survive in an online world because of its standing."

ISSUE NUMBER 5

EXTRAORDINARY SENSATIONS

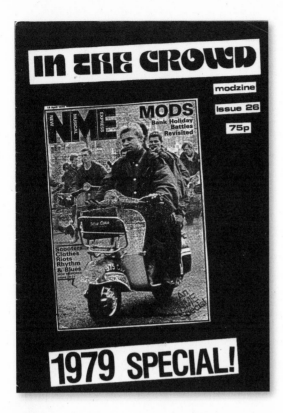

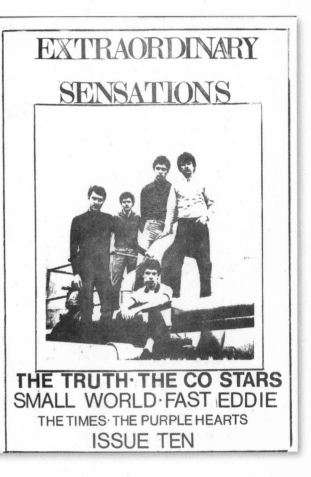

In The Crowd – Derek 'Delboy' Shepherd, Guernsey 1988.
Modculture – David Walker, online 2010 / ongoing.
Extraordinary Sensations – Eddie Piller and Terry Rawlings,
Essex 1983.

Fanzines were once the lifeblood of the worldwide mod scene and were produced in such limited numbers that they have become collectors' items and can be extremely valuable. With the advent of eBay and other auction sites, rare fanzines can fetch large sums of money. In 2004, Issue 3 of **Extraordinary Sensations** sold for well over £100!

Occasionally fanzines have been viewed with academic seriousness. The Kristin Sibley Archive at the Museum of Applied Arts and Sciences, Sydney, is dedicated to home-made mod magazines from 1981 to 1986, the golden period of the Australian scene. On the US West Coast, the San Diego State Special Collections and University Archive holds an enormous fanzine selection. Here in the UK, the British Library archivists also sat up and took notice, going so far as to subscribe to **Extraordinary Sensations** and requesting an entire set of back copies (something which I was sadly unable to provide, since, as I previously mentioned, I no longer hold a copy of Issue 1 in my own personal archive). These three aren't alone; it seems that historians regard not just mod fanzines but all fanzines as an important indicator of trends in social anthropology.

Neil Allen, himself the editor of the Jam-influenced fanzine **Start!**, which ran to eight issues in the nineties, has established the Facebook group Mod Fanzines, where he has scanned and uploaded the majority (but not all) of his extensive collection. Readers of this book are strongly advised to visit the group to discover some of the fanzines that, for space reasons, we haven't been able to feature in this book.

Neil recalls: "In the eighties, I was based in the north-east of England, in an area where there was not much of a local scene. The huge array of mod fanzines and newsletters was a godsend for keeping up to date with what was happening. Whether it was weekly news via **The Phoenix List** or **The Britania**, or regular zines such as **GoGo** and **In The Crowd,** the feeling of being part of an exciting and vibrant world could still be had via this amazing communication network. The mod fanzines were our eighties equivalent of Facebook and other social media! Being a collector (or is it a hoarder?), I kept everything, and then when eBay opened up the memorabilia market, I continued to buy and now have 600–700 different mod fanzines."

Another excellent archive belongs to David 'Dizzy' Holmes' and is published on his Detour Records sister website, **Bored Teenagers**, a site that extolls the virtues of both the 1970s punk scene as well as the mod revival. You can find it at www.boredteenagers.co.uk/MODFANZIES.htm (sic).

Dizzy's label, Detour, has been the mainstay of the mod revival since the 1980s. "Fanzines were more important than the main music press, specifically because they were at a grassroots level, written by fans for fans. They kept you up to date with what was happening on the scene and most, if not all of them, were done for love and not profit. They are also an extremely important social history document because they were written with no frills. They pretty much told the truth…"

Start! – Neil Allen,
West Midlands 1994-1997.

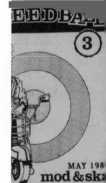

Acknowledgements

Eddie

Firstly, I would like to dedicate this book to both Henry Storch and Sean O'Gorman, two lifelong friends who both sadly passed away shortly after being interviewed for this book.

I would like to thank Terry Rawlings, who was my partner in *Extraordinary Sensations*, and Maxine Conroy, who partnered both of us in our Countdown adventure. Big thanks also go out to my literary agent, Danny Keene, and our editor, Lucy Beevor, whose patience made finishing the manuscript a pleasure. All the people who gave their advice or consented to be interviewed deserve a mention, most especially Dizzy Holmes from Detour, whose *Bored Teenagers* archive was invaluable, and Neil Allen, who has the largest collection of modzines I have ever come across. Finally, I would like to thank Dave Stokes, our long-suffering printer at *Extraordinary Sensations*, without whom none of this would have been possible. I thank you all.

Steve

I would like to thank Eddie Piller for joining me and without whom this book would never have got out of the starting blocks and Danny Keene for getting the vision. Big thanks to Neil Allen for all the support and help from the early days, Derek 'Delboy' Shepherd, Roger Dixon and Dizzy Holmes, for sharing their invaluable archive of fanzines, photos and press cuttings. This book is dedicated to my kids, Declan and Maia, who gave me time to do this book.

Thanks to Goffa Gladding, co-editor of *Maximum Speed,* for kindly giving us permission to reprint Issue One of that illustrious fanzine in the special edition of this book, and Tony Perfect from Long Tall Shorty who facilitated the reissue of the band's 45, originally included as a flexidisc in *Direction Reaction Creation*, as a vinyl single in the same, slipcased edition of the book.

NB: Please note the fanzines in this book are from private collections and have been scanned and improved to the best of our ability.

176